Louisiana

A History

Joe Gray Taylor

**With a Historical Guide
prepared by the editors of
the American Association for
State and Local History**

W. W. Norton & Company
New York · London

American Association for State and Local History
Nashville

In memory of Enoch L. Mitchell

Author and publishers make grateful acknowledgment to the Department of Archives, Louisiana State University, for permission to quote from the R. E. McGuire Diary.

Published and distributed by
W. W. Norton & Company, Inc.
500 Fifth Avenue
New York, New York 10110

Library of Congress Cataloguing-in-Publication Data

Taylor, Joe Gray.
　Louisiana, a history.

　(The States and the Nation series)
　Bibliography: p. 185
　Includes index.
1.　Louisiana—History　I.　Title.　II.　Series.
F369.T29　　　976.3　　　76–24848
ISBN 0-393-30174-5

Printed in the United States of America

1 2 3 4 5 6 7 8 9 0

Contents

ℋistorical Guide

TO LOUISIANA

prepared by the editors of the
American Association for State and Local History

Introduction

The following pages offer the reader a guide to places in this state
through which its history still lives.

This section lists and describes museums with collections of valuable artifacts, historic houses where prominent people once lived, and
historic sites where events of importance took place. In addition, we
have singled out for detailed description a few places that illustrate
especially well major developments in this state's history or major
themes running through it, as identified in the text that follows. The
reader can visit these places to experience what life was like in earlier
times and learn more about the state's rich and exciting heritage.

James B. Gardner and Timothy C. Jacobson, professional historians
on the staff of the American Association for State and Local History,
prepared this supplementary material, and the association's editors take
sole responsibility for the selection of sites and their descriptions.
Nonetheless, thanks are owed to many individuals and historical organizations, including those listed, for graciously providing informa-
tion and advice. Our thanks also go to the National Endowment for
the Humanities, which granted support for the writing and editing of
this supplement, as it did for the main text itself.   —*The Editors*

Louisiana State Museum

New Orleans

★ New Orleans—legendary for jazz, fine food, and Mardi Gras—is unique among Louisiana and American cities. European visitors to America often comment that it is the only one that resembles their own. Not only is it old as American cities go, but it also looks old. Visitors' impressions are shaped, of course, by the fa-

The Cabildo on Jackson Square

mous French Quarter or Vieux Carre, actually only a small enclave within a modern metropolis that itself could hardly remind Europeans of home. To most American tourists, too, New Orleans means the French Quarter, its exotic tastes and entertainments unlike anything back home and therefore especially alluring.

But the French Quarter is rightly known as far more than a pleasure emporium. How it looks, not just what it sells, truly distinguishes it. Though the entire Vieux Carre Historic District (as the French Quarter is officially designated) contains hundreds of distinctive balconied buildings that are festooned with wrought iron and surround quiet tropical courtyards, the properties of the Louisiana State Museum are among the best preserved. They offer the history-minded visitor to this exotic place an exceptional sample of architectural history and, through it, the history of early New Orleans. Several are open to the public. None, ironically, is technically French, nor are many of the buildings anywhere in the quarter. New Orleans' history has not been so simple.

The French began it, and their influence endures today over a century and three-quarters after the city passed for the last time from their hands. In between much happened, as these historic buildings testify. The early years under the French rule were hardly auspicious. Founded in 1718 under the auspices of the Company of the Indies by Jean Baptiste le Moyne Sieur de Bienville at the place where the Mississippi River and Lake Pontchartrain came closest together, New Orleans was not the first settlement in Louisiana, though it would be the greatest. But greatness was a long way off, and for many years this place grandly named for the Duke of Orleans remained a rude frontier town on the edge of a subtropical wilderness.

Louisiana generally was not a place conducive to easy settlement. Control switched back and forth between the French government and several proprietary companies, all of whom encountered considerable frustration in trying to make Louisiana work. All of them also lost money. To populate the place convicts and prostitutes were sent forcibly from France. When their presence failed to have a sustaining effect, large grants were offered to concessionaires if they could import French agricultural tenants who at least could raise enough food to feed themselves. Good farmers finally were found in war-wracked Germany; many were enticed to Louisiana, and many prospered there. From Africa and the West Indies came slaves, and while they too stayed, they hardly prospered. Though by the 1740s some of the rougher edges had been worn off, the best New Orleans had to offer still could not have been very impressive. It counted probably less than 4,000 whites (800 of whom were soldiers), 2,000 slaves, and a few free blacks. It was not yet a prosperous trading city because the hinterland did not yet produce much that found a ready market in France.

The city's next sovereigns, the Spanish, enjoyed more luck—if only because settlement throughout eastern North America was more secure by the late eighteenth century, and trade coming down the Mississippi River at last made real the long-suspected potential of the town that controlled its mouth. After the Pinckney Treaty of 1795 between Spain and the new American nation gave the United States the right of deposit in New Orleans, the hides, meat, flour, and whiskey of half a continent came floating down to New Orleans. Vigorous Spanish administration and generous land grants finally sparked a tremendous increase in population, and by the late 1790s the successful cultivation of sugar cane and cotton were beginning to make of the Louisiana economy what it would be for years to come.

Thanks to the vagaries of European politics, sovereignty over Louisiana passed briefly back to France in 1800 and three years later (in what has been widely described ever since as the greatest real estate deal in history) to the young United States for the sum of $15 million, or about four cents an acre (the boundaries were somewhat vague). It has remained American (or Confederate) ever since and has grown and prospered with the nation. With them the Americans brought new ways of government and some other new ways of thinking and behaving. With them, as the years passed, New Orleans' and Louisiana's already mixed population and culture made its own distinctive accommodation, as the architecture of the French Quarter reveals. What French buildings there once were, however, were destroyed in the fires that swept the original town in 1788 and 1794, and what we now commonly call French is actually Spanish. The two premier buildings of the Louisiana State Museum properties are excellent examples.

The Cabildo, a massive three-story structure of stuccoed brick, was built between 1795 and 1799, very near the end of Spanish rule. But the Spanish built well, and what once housed their governing council of Louisiana became briefly the French *Maison de Ville*, then public offices under the Americans, and in 1911 the Louisiana State Museum. In its Sala Capitular the French formally transferred New Orleans and Louisiana to the United States. Today the Cabildo houses exhibitions on the settlement of Louisiana during the French, Spanish, and early American periods. On the third floor (a steep-sided mansard roof addition from the 1850s) is the Mississippi River Gallery, which examines the place of that great river in the history of Louisiana and New Orleans.

The Presbytère, flanking St. Louis Cathedral on the other side from the Cabildo, gives the appearance of being the Cabildo's twin, though it was built for a different purpose and is several years older. It was never used as originally intended—as the cathedral rectory—but was leased for commercial shops and during the nineteenth century housed the Louisiana Supreme Court. Today it contains numerous exhibits, including the Louisiana Portrait Gallery. Together, the Presbytère and the Cabildo make one of the most imposing museums in the country and an enduring reminder of the Spanish presence in New Orleans.

Another museum property, located nearby on Dumaine Street, reveals the Spanish period in a different light. Madame John's Legacy (named for a fictitious character linked with the house in a short story by George Washington Cable) is a colonial raised cottage built in the late 1780s. Outside it is restored to its original appearance; inside its galleries and period rooms hold a fine collection of colonial Louisiana furniture and decorative arts. Two other more modest residences dating from the American period are the Creole House in Pirate's Alley and the Jackson House on St. Peter Street. The Creole House, built in 1842 on the site of an old colonial prison, displays the shuttered windows, balconies, and delicate wrought iron that have come to symbolize New Orleans. It is now home for the Friends of the Cabildo. The Jackson House (named for the hero of the Battle of New Orleans), also built in 1842, is of similar appearance and houses additional museum galleries. Just a few doors away, on the site of the Spanish arsenal, stands the American arsenal, built in 1839 and acquired by the State Museum in 1915. When restored it will house transportation and military collections.

After the Cabildo and the Presbytère, the museum's two most imposing properties are the Lower Pontalba and the United States Mint. The Mint, located at the east end of the Quarter just a block from the river, was built in 1835 during the first presidential term of Andrew Jackson and is today the oldest surviving mint building in the United States. It was also the only mint of the Confederacy. Coinage was minted behind its red brick walls and massive white columns until 1909. Before its recent restoration by the State Museum it served in a number of other roles. The Lower Pontalba on Jackson Square, though comparable in size to the Mint, could hardly be more different in every other respect. The long red brick block between Chartres and Decatur on Jackson Square (and its duplicate across the square) was built by the Baroness Micaela Almonester de Pontalba in 1850 to provide elegant residences on the upper two floors and shops on the street level. The State Museum's 1850 home, in the Lower Pontalba, offers visitors a glimpse of what elegant urban living was like just before the Civil War, during New Orleans' most prosperous era. High ceilings, balconies, fine woodwork, and servants' quarters and private courtyards at the rear distinguished the Lower Pontalba even in a city famous for elegant residences. Today there are still shops on the ground floor, and a section houses the Louisiana State Museum historical research library.

For the visitor to New Orleans' French Quarter, there are many popular attractions. These buildings are perhaps not its most famous. But for the visitor with an eye for historically revealing architecture, they are an excellent place to start exploring the past of this unique place. They are all within easy walking distance of one another. And walking itself is one of the French Quarter's extra rewards.

Chalmette Battlefield

Chalmette

★ America's first years as a new nation were not easy ones. The military victory that achieved independence from Great Britain was followed by a number of domestic trials. The first system of American government—the Articles of Confederation—proved a dismal failure. The federal

Chalmette Battlefield

Constitution that replaced them, though it survived in the long run, sparked bitter debate and dissension in the beginning. The first system of political parties was established only with much labor and acrimony, and during the crisis over the Alien and Sedition Acts in the late 1790s it appeared that the very idea of a loyal opposition might not survive.

Nor did the winning of independence mean that other nations respected the new republic or expected it to endure. The beaten British were far from friendly; and while recognition did come from them and other European powers, none could much sympathize with the principles behind the new American experiment in popular government. The French, America's vital wartime allies, were soon beset by their own revolution, which, as it grew more radical in the 1790s and degenerated into a military dictatorship, alienated much American opinion. And that Revolution soon spread war once again over much of Europe. France under Napoleon dominated the land; Britain ruled the seas. They were locked in mortal struggle more or less constantly for twenty years.

One might have thought that the Great Powers, thus preoccupied with each other, would have left America, remote and harmless far across the Atlantic, well enough alone. But the United States then was very much a maritime nation. Disputes over shipping and neutral rights led to an undeclared naval war with France between 1798 and 1800 and to Thomas Jefferson's ill-fated Embargo of 1807–1809 whereby he sought to use economic pressure to bring the belligerents to terms. He failed; and as the European war dragged on, Britain through her powerful Royal Navy trespassed more and more on American commerce. The specific issue was impressment: the seizure of sailors (many of whom, the British claimed, were British subjects) from American ships for forced service in the Royal Navy. The larger issue, of course, was respect for the American flag: whether the young republic had yet really achieved independence. On land, the British still controlled the vast reaches of Canada, where—according to Henry Clay and other American "War Hawks" in 1810 and 1811—they fomented Indian raids on the frontier. Had not the time come to eliminate the British from North America altogether?

The War of 1812, fought between a badly divided United States (in New England, which lived by trade, there was talk of secession) and a battle-weary Britain, decided it. For the Americans it was a poorly run affair. The navy was small; the regular army was inexperienced and badly administered. Early campaigns to drive into Canada were disasters. The American garrison at Fort Dearborn (future Chicago) was massacred; Detroit fell to the British without a fight; a plan to attack Montreal pitifully fizzled. At sea the news was better, as American seamanship and some skilled commanders bloodied the British in several memorable engagements. But through 1813 neither side could strike a decisive blow.

In April of 1814, however, the overthrow of Napoleon in Europe enabled the British to concentrate new resources on the troublesome war with their old American colonies. Fourteen thousand veterans of the Duke of Wellington's campaigns crossed the Atlantic to finish the business. It was not an easy job. Along the Niagara frontier both sides fought fiercely; Chippewa and Lundy's Lane became famous battle-grounds. On Lake Champlain American naval forces won an important victory, but after the loss of Fort Erie opposite Buffalo in November the Americans abandoned their drive on Canada for good. To the south the British mounted secondary actions in the Chesapeake Bay region and in August, 1814, inflicted on the Americans perhaps their greatest humiliation. British troops captured Washington and burned the Capitol and the White House. At Baltimore they met stiffer resistance and finally were stopped at Fort McHenry. Withdrawing to Jamaica, the British prepared for the action that left so many of them dead at Chalmette.

The capture of New Orleans, the British strategists reasoned, would give them control of the entire Mississippi Valley. If they succeeded they could strangle the outlet for western produce that came down the Ohio and Mississippi rivers and effectively dispute American power over the vast lands of Jefferson's Louisiana Purchase. With the stakes so high, they committed much to the effort: fifty ships and an army of 10,000 men sailed from Jamaica for the Gulf Coast. They looked invincible.

But they figured without Andrew Jackson, the American general in charge of the southern frontier, whose ability to rally the diverse and contentious population of New Orleans turned looming disaster into a great victory. The British approached stealthily by way of Lake Borgne and got within nine miles of New Orleans before they were discovered by the Americans. A disconcerted Jackson quickly attacked the gathering British force at the Villère Plantation on December 23, 1814. Though the confused night action was indecisive, it momentarily stalled the British advance and gave the Americans time to organize their real defense of the Crescent City.

For that purpose Jackson chose the Chalmette Plantation three miles upriver from Villère's. The invaders had to pass this way, and it offered good defensive ground. He established his line along the Rodriquez Canal, a shallow ditch along which he hurriedly constructed a shoulder-high rampart of mud and fence-rails. With his flanks protected by the river on the right and an impassable cypress swamp on the left, he had only to meet his enemy head-on. Behind this fortification Jackson gathered his motley army. With him from Tennessee came a loyal band of frontiersmen and Indian fighters, who with other volunteers from Kentucky, Mississippi, and Louisiana formed the core of his command. But he swelled their ranks with black refugees from the Caribbean, Choctaw Indians, released convicts, and—most legendary of all—Jean Lafitte's buccaneers from Barataria Bay. Their ranks totalled roughly 5,000, half the strength of their opponents.

The test came on January 8, 1815, and the result was the most one-sided victory in American military history. Jackson's defenders, many of them excellent marksmen armed with long rifles, commanded a clear field of fire over the Chalmette plantation; along the American line there were also eight batteries of artillery. To the skirl of Scottish Highlanders' bagpipes, the British bravely advanced in rank order, only to be cut down by a withering American fire. With enormous discipline they attacked Jackson's rampart three times. The British general, Edward Packenham, and his second in command were both killed, and in just two hours their force suffered over 2,000 casualties. The Americans lost just seven killed and six wounded. Jackson did not take the offensive, but within ten days the beaten British army left Louisiana forever.

Unbeknownst to any of the combatants, a peace treaty ending the war had been signed in Ghent, Belgium, on Christmas Eve, 1814. Thus this greatest of American land victories had no effect on the war's outcome. But it mattered for other reasons. For the young American nation, the stunning defeat of the British boosted national morale and was a fitting end to a frustrating and divisive war. It made of Andrew Jackson—destined to become president of the United States and a symbol for the age of the common man—a national hero. And it confirmed in the eyes of England and the rest of the world the permanence of the American national experiment. The Battle of New Orleans was also the last battle ever fought between Britain and the United States, two countries that thereafter peacefully went their separate ways. History in time brought them together on other fields of battle—but never again as foes.

Rural Life Museum

Baton Rouge

★ Of all the southern states, Louisiana may be the most extraordinary. At least its historical image is the most exotic. The familiar antebellum legend of gallant gentlemen, gentle ladies, faithful retainers, all set against a backdrop of white columns, becomes in Louisiana especially seductive. Louisiana

Plantation commissary

historian Joe Gray Taylor writes: "[T]he handsome gentlemen may be speaking French, and the ladies, answering in the same romantic tongue, are small, dark, and vivacious, possessed of all the virtues of their Anglo-Saxon sisters elsewhere in the South, but with the spicy tang of Latinism added." The setting and the supporting cast too are better: "Away from the Big House and the slave quarter stretch endless cotton and cane fields, surrounded by trees bowed down with Spanish moss, and here and there a cabin from which comes the sound of a fiddle playing an Acadian tune, sung by a large, happy illiterate family in an appealing patois." Romantic Hollywood movies once were made with such casts and sets. Part fact and part fiction, it is a tenacious image.

More recently, however, it has been fashionable among historians to debunk the image. It portrays, they argue, the way only a few fortunate Louisianians lived and masks the misery and injustice that was the lot of many whites and most blacks. Perhaps so. But not all the power of the image derives from its romantic trimmings. If it errs in some of its particulars, it is also correct on one of the most important points: it portrays a culture that was profoundly and enduringly rural. The nature of that ruralism could vary considerably. On the rich black alluvial soil that reaches from the Arkansas border down the west bank of the Mississippi, along both banks below the mouth of the Red River and along Bayou Lafourche and Bayou Teche, plantations, some not unlike the romantic image, once flourished. To the north they raised cotton or sugar; south Louisiana was sugar country.

Despite the presence of the great port city of New Orleans and the thousands of Louisianians who were not planters, these plantations dominated the state in the antebellum era. On the eve of the Civil War there were some 1,600 plantations with more than fifty slaves each. Tensas Parish alone counted 118. New Orleans itself was an old-fashioned commercial city whose gentry and thriving middle class serviced the needs of the countryside and profited from handling its products. It moved to rural rhythms, its bankers and merchants busiest during the fall and winter when the plantations' harvest arrived by steamboat from upriver. Probably the most important figure in the city's economy was the cotton or sugar "factor," the planters' business agent in New Orleans. His job was to get the best possible price for the crop and to handle the purchase of supplies needed on the plantations. On the sale of the crop he received a commission, usually two to three percent, and he collected interest on the unpaid balance of accounts carried for his customers. The countryside, too, was dominated by the great plantations. Those 1,600 with at least fifty slaves apiece covered over forty-three percent of the state's arable land, and the many more with at least twenty bondsmen covered an even larger area.

Still, there were many rural people who were not planters. The majority of white Louisiana farmers were more or less prosperous yeomen who worked the soil with their own hands and perhaps the labor of a slave or two. Though they may have planted small amounts of cotton or sugar cane to bring in cash, they were essentially subsistence farmers who raised corn and livestock to support their families. They far outnumbered planters in the hills of northern Louisiana and in the eastern parts of the Florida parishes. The blacks, who were half the people of the state, were also largely rural and nearly all slaves. For them, plantations and even smaller farms meant something different from what they did for the whites. And there were many whites who existed above, but not much above, the mudsill status of the slaves. Poor and landless, they grew in numbers as time went on.

After the Civil War, much changed in Louisiana and the rest of the South. Most notably, slavery disappeared; but, contrary to much popular belief, the plantations did not go with it. Agriculture in the South as elsewhere was growing more commercialized, and landholdings continued to be consolidated in a trend begun before the war. The yeomen as a class lost most. Lack of credit forced them to become dependent on the crop lien system. In time, as they were driven hopelessly into debt, many lost their land and became sharecroppers. The crop lien was an expedient brought about by the reduced value of farmland after the war and the inability of farmers to use it as security for credit. Instead they were forced to use their crops, on which their creditors (frequently the crossroads merchant who sold seed and other farm and household supplies) took a lien or mortgage. The farmer's security was a crop still being grown or perhaps still planned. If it failed to materialize—and the possibility of failure due to sickness, insects, floods, or cold weather was ever present—the consequences could be disastrous. At best the farmer paid dearly for his credit (''from twenty-five percent to grand larceny,'' it was said).

Sharecropping, meanwhile, began as a transition from slave to free labor, but it ended as an entrenched system of labor for many blacks and whites in the cottonfields. Essentially a substitute for wages, it worked simply enough. Planters who needed labor but could not pay cash for it offered instead a cabin, work stock, tools, seed—and a share in the crops—to the tenants. Tenants bought their own food and supplies from a plantation nommissary, on credit because they had no cash, and paid at year's end with the proceeds from their share of the crop. If they owed more than their share covered and went into debt, laws prevented them from moving without the creditor's permission. It was a necessary system initially but one that unfortunately perpetuated itself over several generations.

Today much has changed. Agriculture since World War II has, like so much else, grown modern. The size of holdings still increases and new crops like soybeans outpace old ones like cotton and sugar. Mechanization has spread and fewer hands raise more. Many of the rural people have moved to town, many out of Louisiana altogether. Thus the LSU Rural Life Museum in Baton Rouge is an especially valuable historical resource. In its extensive collection of tools, furniture, and farm implements, today's visitor, who very likely comes from a city, can recapture something of the rural world that most Lousianians, whether rich or poor, once knew.

This major outdoor folk museum spreads over five acres of plantation and includes more than fifteen buildings. There are three distinct areas.

The Barn is an exhibit hall containing the museum's extensive collection of artifacts. These range from a bale of cotton picked and baled by slaves in the early 1860s to a collection of textile machines used in the homes of the nineteenth century; woodworking and blacksmithing tools; and displays on lumbering, hunting, and trapping, all common activities of rural dwellers years ago. The Working Plantation illustrates that part of plantation life that is hidden behind the elegant antebellum mansions; this is what made those mansions possible. With the exception of the blacksmith shop and the sugarhouse, all are original nineteenth-century structures. A plantation commissary dating from the 1880s was once a busy general store for sharecroppers. The overseer's house features original *bousillage* walls, a unique Louisiana building technique by which hand-hewn cypress was coated on the inside with a mixture of mud and Spanish moss and then plastered. The Sick House was once a slave cabin, of which there are several others on the Plantation. The Schoolhouse is furnished with bench-type desks, notebooks, and slates, as it would have been when the children of overseers and yeoman farmers learned their lessons here. The schoolbooks date from the 1870s; notebooks contain French lessons. A cane-grinder and a sugar house recall a key process in sugar manufacturing that once was done on the plantation where the cane itself was raised.

Finally, the museum's collection of folk architecture preserves some of the non-farm buildings once familiar in rural Louisiana. A country church recalls similar structures all over the South. Three of the most common styles of rural house are also on display. The dogtrot house, with its front and rear porches and twin chimneys, is typical of north Louisiana (and much of the rest of the South). The Acadian or Creole house recalls the French-speaking settlers in the southern part of the state. An outside stairway leads to a second-floor room where part of the family slept. In the museum's shotgun house, the rooms are placed distinctively one behind the other. As the attentive visitor no doubt will notice, only the white-columned plantation house is missing. That is by design. Plantation houses (some very much in keeping with the romantic image of the Old South) still abound in Louisiana, and a few actually still are lived in by planters. The LSU Rural Live Museum preserves another rural South—that of both the ordinary people who supported life in the "Big House" and those who aspired to it.

Other Places of Interest

*The following suggest other places of
historical interest to visit. We recommend that
you check hours of operation in advance.*

AUDUBON STATE COMMEMORATIVE AREA, *state 965 east of St.
Francisville.* Receives its name from a short stay by artist John James Audubon in 1821; includes colonial house, "Oakley," built in 1799.

THE COTTAGE PLANTATION. *U.S. 61 at Cottage Lane, St. Francisville.*
Complete early-nineteenth-century plantation with French Colonial house
started in 1795.

DESTRAHAN PLANTATION, *River Road (state 48), Destrahan.* A plantation originally devoted to growing indigo and sugar, built in 1787 and representative of area colonial architecture.

E. D. WHITE STATE COMMEMORATIVE AREA, *five miles north of Thibodaux on state highway 1.* A park with the birthplace and home, built
about 1790, of a U.S. Supreme Court justice who participated in rulings on
the Sherman Antitrust Act in 1911.

FAUBOURG MARIGNY HISTORIC DISTRICT, *bounded by Esplanade Avenue, Press Street, St. Claude Avenue, and the Mississippi River, New Orleans.* Many residences in the Creole, Greek Revival, Victorian, and Edwardian styles.

FORT JACKSON, *state 23, Buras.* A bastioned brick pentagon begun in 1822,
active in the Civil War, and used until 1920.

FORT JESUP STATE COMMEMORATIVE AREA, *state 6 northeast of
Many.* One original log building remaining of a United States military post
established in 1822 on El Camino Real (San Antonio Trace), along with
replica of officers' quarters and a museum.

FORT PIKE STATE COMMEMORATIVE AREA, *U.S. 90E north of New
Orleans.* Partially restored brick fort built 1819–1821, with historical exhibits on the War of 1812 and the Civil War.

FORT POLK MILITARY MUSEUM, *Building 917, South Carolina Avenue,
Fort Polk.* A museum with collections from World War II to the present.

GALLIER HALL, *545 St. Charles Avenue, New Orleans.* The 1850 Greek
Revival New Orleans City Hall designed by James Gallier, Sr.

GALLIER HOUSE, *1132 Royal Street, New Orleans.* House built 1857–1860 with Renaissance Revival and local French elements, and a museum.

HISTORIC NEW ORLEANS COLLECTION, *533 Royal Street,* New Orleans. A museum of paintings, maps, and other articles related to Louisiana life, located in the 1792 Merieult House.

HOUMAS HOUSE, *River Road (state highway 942), Burnside.* Greek Revival mansion built in 1840 onto late-eighteenth-century sections; the setting for several movies.

IMPERIAL CALCASIEU MUSEUM, *204 W. Sallier Street, Lake Charles.* Furnishings and other items from the Victorian period.

KENT HOUSE STATE COMMEMORATIVE AREA, *Bayou Rapides at Virginia Avenue, west of Alexandria.* A country plantation built in 1796 with later additions, reflecting Creole influence; with gardens and antique furnishings.

LONGFELLOW-EVANGELINE STATE COMMEMORATIVE AREA, *state 31, St. Martinville.* An Acadian house built in 1765; with a museum of Acadian crafts.

LOWER GARDEN DISTRICT, *bounded by Mississippi River, Phillips Street, Saint Charles Avenue, Annunciation Street, Race Street, and U.S. 90, New Orleans.* Nineteenth-century residential and commercial buildings with park, canals, and fountains.

MADEWOOD PLANTATION HOUSE, *Bayou Lafourche facing state 308, Napoleonville.* Greek Revival house, built 1840–1848; with antebellum fixtures and furnishings.

MAGNOLIA MOUND PLANTATION, *2161 Nicholson Drive, Baton Rouge.* Restored late-eighteenth-century house with Federal-period furnishings.

MANSFIELD BATTLE PARK, *state 175 southeast of Mansfield.* Museum with Civil War artifacts on site of 1864 battle where Confederates stopped Union soldiers in Red River campaign.

MARKSVILLE STATE COMMEMORATIVE AREA, *state 5, Marksville.* Museum on site of Indian mounds, earliest from the pre-Christian era; with artifacts from the mounds.

MARSTON HOUSE, *Bank Street, Clinton.* An 1838 Greek Revival house used as a hospital during the Civil War; open by appointment.

MELROSE PLANTATION, *state highway 119 just east of junction with 493, Melrose.* Several houses, oldest dating from 1830s and some with possibly African design, built by free blacks over several decades.

THE MYRTLES PLANTATION, *state 61, St. Francisville.* Begun in 1796 by Gen. David Bradford, who led the Whiskey Rebellion in Pennsylvania; with antiques and furnishings of the early 1800s.

NATCHITOCHES HISTORIC DISTRICT, *bounded by College Avenue and Texas, Third, and Front streets, and including the Williams Avenue area east of Cane River-Lake, Natchitoches.* In an area where French established fort in 1714; oldest permanent settlement in Louisiana, containing buildings from 1700s to 1900s.

OAK ALLEY PLANTATION, *Great River Road west of Vacherie.* House built by French sugar planter 1837–1839 on site where early French settler had planted twenty-eight live oaks in rows—now leading up to Greek Revival house with twenty-eight Doric columns.

OLD STATE CAPITOL, *North Boulevard and River Road, Baton Rouge.* Gothic Revival castle built in 1849, now housing art exhibits and visitors bureau.

OLD URSULINE CONVENT, *1114 Chartres Street, New Orleans.* Built in 1745 and one of the few buildings with authentic French architecture remaining in New Orleans.

PARLANGE PLANTATION, *junction of state 1 and 78, Mix.* Built about 1750, one of the finest examples of the French Colonial "raised cottage" type of house.

PIONEER HERITAGE CENTER, *Louisiana State University in Shreveport, Shreveport.* Authentic recreation of the pioneer culture of northwest Louisiana, 1830–1860.

PORT HUDSON BATTLEFIELD, *along U.S. 61, Port Hudson.* Earthworks where free blacks and ex-slaves fought Confederate soldiers in 1863.

POVERTY POINT STATE COMMEMORATIVE AREA, *state 557 north of Epps.* Unique mound and ridge complex of pre-Christian era, with museum containing artifacts from the site.

ROSEDOWN, *state 10 north of St. Francisville.* An 1835 mansion with extensive gardens inspired by French style.

ST. CHARLES STREETCAR LINE, *New Orleans.* Laid out in 1835 on the route on St. Charles Avenue to Carrollton; still operates with cars built in the 1920s.

ST. LOUIS CATHEDRAL, *Jackson Square, New Orleans.* Begun in 1789 and enlarged in the mid-nineteenth century; still in use.

SHADOWS-ON-THE-TECHE, *117 E. Main Street, New Iberia.* Greek Revival house built 1831–1834.

STATE CAPITOL, *downtown Baton Rouge.* Built 1931–1932, a 450-foot-tall building inspired by Governor Huey P. Long; with murals in the foyer and an observation tower on top.

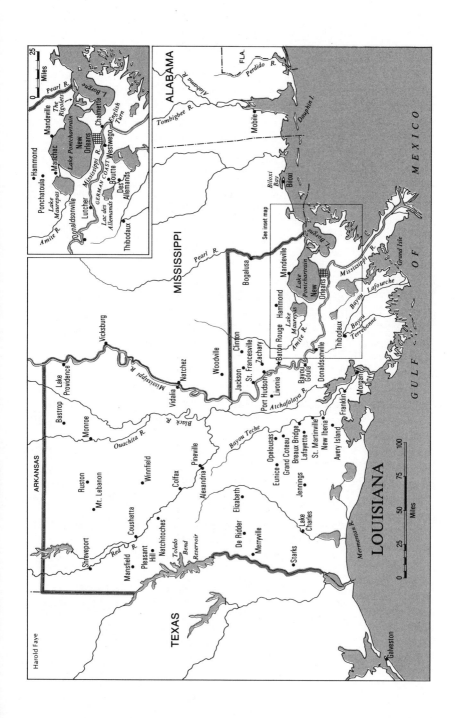

Harold Faye

Invitation to the Reader

IN 1807, former President John Adams argued that a complete history of the American Revolution could not be written until the history of change in each state was known, because the principles of the Revolution were as various as the states that went through it. Two hundred years after the Declaration of Independence, the American nation has spread over a continent and beyond. The states have grown in number from thirteen to fifty. And democratic principles have been interpreted differently in every one of them.

We therefore invite you to consider that the history of your state may have more to do with the bicentennial review of the American Revolution than does the story of Bunker Hill or Valley Forge. The Revolution has continued as Americans extended liberty and democracy over a vast territory. John Adams was right: the states are part of that story, and the story is incomplete without an account of their diversity.

The Declaration of Independence stressed life, liberty, and the pursuit of happiness; accordingly, it shattered the notion of holding new territories in the subordinate status of colonies. The Northwest Ordinance of 1787 set forth a procedure for new states to enter the Union on an equal footing with the old. The Federal Constitution shortly confirmed this novel means of building a nation out of equal states. The step-by-step process through which territories have achieved self-government and national representation is among the most important of the Founding Fathers' legacies.

The method of state-making reconciled the ancient conflict between liberty and empire, resulting in what Thomas Jefferson called an empire for liberty. The system has worked and remains unaltered, despite enormous changes that have taken

place in the nation. The country's extent and variety now sur-
pass anything the patriots of '76 could likely have imagined.
The United States has changed from an agrarian republic into a
highly industrial and urban democracy, from a fledgling nation
into a major world power. As Oliver Wendell Holmes remarked
in 1920, the creators of the nation could not have seen completely how it and its constitution and its states would develop.
Any meaningful review in the bicentennial era must consider
what the country has become, as well as what it was.

The new nation of equal states took as its motto *E Pluribus
Unum*—"out of many, one." But just as many peoples have
become Americans without complete loss of ethnic and cultural
identities, so have the states retained differences of character.
Some have been superficial, expressed in stereotyped images—
big, boastful Texas, "sophisticated" New York, "hillbilly"
Arkansas. Other differences have been more real, sometimes instructively, sometimes amusingly; democracy has embraced
Huey Long's Louisiana, bilingual New Mexico, unicameral Ne-
braska, and a Texas that once taxed fortunetellers and spawned
politicians called "Woodpecker Republicans" and "Skunk
Democrats." Some differences have been profound, as when
South Carolina secessionists led other states out of the Union in
opposition to abolitionists in Massachusetts and Ohio. The result was a bitter Civil War.

The Revolution's first shots may have sounded in Lexington
and Concord; but fights over what democracy should mean and
who should have independence have erupted from Pennsylvania's Gettysburg to the "Bleeding Kansas" of John Brown,
from the Alamo in Texas to the Indian battles at Montana's
Little Bighorn. Utah Mormons have known the strain of isolation; Hawaiians at Pearl Harbor, the terror of attack; Georgians
during Sherman's march, the sadness of defeat and devastation.
Each state's experience differs instructively; each adds understanding to the whole.

The purpose of this series of books is to make that kind of understanding accessible, in a way that will last in value far
beyond the bicentennial fireworks. The series offers a volume
on every state, plus the District of Columbia—fifty-one, in all.

Each book contains, besides the text, a view of the state through eyes other than the author's—a "photographer's essay," in which a skilled photographer presents his own personal perceptions of the state's contemporary flavor.

We have asked authors not for comprehensive chronicles, nor for research monographs or new data for scholars. Bibliographies and footnotes are minimal. We have asked each author for a summing up—interpretive, sensitive, thoughtful, individual, even personal—of what seems significant about his or her state's history. What distinguishes it? What has mattered about it, to its own people and to the rest of the nation? What has it come to now?

To interpret the states in all their variety, we have sought a variety of backgrounds in authors themselves and have encouraged variety in the approaches they take. They have in common only these things: historical knowledge, writing skill, and strong personal feelings about a particular state. Each has wide latitude for the use of the short space. And if each succeeds, it will be by offering you, in your capacity as a *citizen* of a state *and* of a nation, stimulating insights to test against your own.

James Morton Smith
General Editor

ACKNOWLEDGMENTS

The list of those who have contributed indirectly to this book would include my fellow graduate students of a little more than a quarter century ago, the teachers who aroused a Tennessee student's interest in Louisiana, and my many associates, academic and otherwise, in the Louisiana Historical Association over the years. The list would also include many of my own students whose questions led me to explore areas I might otherwise have ignored.

More specifically, I must especially acknowledge R. A. Suarez of McNeese State University, who read each chapter as it was written, who did not hesitate to point out errors of fact, and who did not always approve of my interpretations. My secretary, Mrs. Marjorie T. Turko, not only typed the manuscript but also served as a most necessary check upon grammar and spelling. My wife, who put up with the burden of a writer who keeps a most disorderly desk, did more than her part. Finally, Gerald George read the early chapters and pointed me in the way I should go.

The responsibility for any errors of fact and for all interpretations is mine and mine alone.

March 1976   *Joe Gray Taylor*

Louisiana

A History

1

Colonial Louisiana: A
Study in Failure

N late 1698, four ships sailed from France under the
command of Pierre le Moyne, Sieur d'Iberville. Aboard
were some two hundred people destined to become the
first settlers of a French post on the lower Mississippi River.
Iberville landed first at Dauphin Island, near modern Mobile,
then moved farther east to Ship Island. From that base he and
his brother, Jean Baptiste, Sieur de Bienville, led a party that
discovered one of the mouths of the Mississippi. Sailing up the
great river, Iberville visited with the Bayou Goula Indians on
the west bank, then sighted a painted pole a little farther upstream on the east bank. That spot he called Baton Rouge. Farther upriver the explorers found the swollen Mississippi cutting
across the base of one of the many bends that mark its course to
the sea. To that spot they gave the name Pointe Coupee, Cut-
Off Point, and the area thereabout is Pointe Coupee Parish to
this day. Iberville took his settlers ashore on the east side of
Biloxi Bay, opposite the site of present-day Biloxi, and built
Fort Maurepas.

Thus began France's second major venture in North American colonization. It would last for sixty-three years and end in
political and economic failure. The colony would suffer from
mistaken policies, neglect, internal strife, corruption, and

threats from outside. When the time came, the French government would turn Louisiana over to Spain with a sigh of relief. Yet France would leave a cultural imprint that would almost completely dominate Spanish Louisiana, that continues to have great influence almost a century and three quarters after Louisiana became part of the United States.

In a sense, the small, hardly defensible Fort Maurepas was the culmination of almost a century of French effort in North America. Quebec had been settled in 1608, and despite hunger and hardship, the colony survived. Missionary zeal and the profits of the fur trade lured priests and *coureurs de bois* up the St. Lawrence River and across the Great Lakes. By 1670, missionaries at Sault Sainte Marie at the outlet of Lake Superior and at Green Bay on the western side of Lake Michigan were working to save heathen souls; traders in the same areas were seeking to profit from the heathens' furs. From the Indians, the French heard of a great river to the west, and in 1673, a trader named Louis Joliet and a Jesuit priest called Père Marquette made their way from Green Bay to the Mississippi and on southward to the mouth of the Arkansas.

René Robert Cavelier, Sieur de La Salle, was a wealthy immigrant to Canada who heard of the voyage of Marquette and Joliet and comprehended the strategic significance of a fort at the mouth of the Mississippi. La Salle knew that the English colonies already established on the Atlantic Coast were thriving; Massachusetts alone had many times the population of all Canada. Soon the entire coast between Florida and Canada would be populated by Englishmen. If a strong French settlement could be established near the river's mouth and then linked with posts farther north, the British could be confined to the lands east of the Appalachians, and the great heartland of the continent would become French.

During the winter of 1682, La Salle led an expedition of fifty-six persons, including ten Indian women and three children, down the Mississippi to its mouth. He reached salt water on April 6, placed a cross in the mud, and claimed the country for France. He gave it the name Louisiana, in honor of King Louis XIV. That was the basis for France's claim to Louisiana, though the Spanish explorer Hernando De Soto had discovered the Mississippi and crossed it 140 years earlier. La Salle returned to Canada and then went to France seeking royal support for a colony on the lower river.

La Salle's ambitions complemented the mercantilist policies of Louis XIV's government. Jean Baptiste Colbert, the king's great finance minister, had recently died, but his belief that colonies contributed to the wealth, prestige, and power of the nation that held them was still strong at the French court. La Salle received the authority he sought, though he was to pay most of the expense of the effort from his own fortune. Thus both strategic and economic considerations led to France's decision to establish a colony near the mouth of the Mississippi.

La Salle's attempt ended in tragedy. His navigation was so poor that his settlers were landed on the coast of Texas. La Salle himself was murdered by his own men as he tried to make his way overland to Canada to find help. The settlement disappeared, victim of starvation, Indians, or Spaniards, but the idea of a colony on the Gulf of Mexico did not perish. It was promoted by Louis Phélypeaux, Count de Pontchartrain, who became Minister of Marine in 1690, and it gathered more strength in 1697 when Henri de Tonti, who had been La Salle's friend, published a book entitled *La Salle's Last Discoveries in America*.

So it was that thirteen years after La Salle's failure, Iberville was selected to lead another attempt. Iberville was one of eleven sons of Charles le Moyne, a Norman who had emigrated to Canada, made a fortune, and been granted a title of nobility. Iberville had earned a distinguished reputation as a naval officer in King William's War, and it was appropriate that he be selected to command the colonizing expedition. Many of the settlers who went with him on that first expedition were Canadians, and it was those men, accustomed to life in the wilderness, who would make the difference between survival and oblivion for the new colony in the early years. Even so, it was a near thing.

From the erection of Fort Maurepas in 1699 until 1712, survival was as much as the colonists could hope for. Even in surviving, however, the colony accomplished a primary purpose, at least for a time. In late 1699, while Iberville returned to France for supplies and more colonists, Bienville made another exploring trip up the Mississippi. As he came back toward the Gulf, he met a British ship that was in the river looking for a spot where a British settlement might be located. Bienville informed the Britisher that he was leading the advance party of a large French naval force. The scene of that encounter has been known ever since as English Turn, because the British ship turned about and sailed back into the Gulf and out of Louisiana history. One can only speculate as to what course Louisiana history might have taken had an English settlement been planted on the lower Mississippi in the early eighteenth century, but certainly it would have been different.

Iberville made the round trip from the Gulf Coast to France twice more, but despite the arrival by way of the Mississippi of Henri de Tonti and other Canadians, settlers died as fast as they arrived. Fort Maurepas was abandoned, and a new post, Fort Louis de Mobile, was established on Mobile Bay. The first site was subject to flooding, however, and in 1711 the fort was located at the site of the present city of Mobile. In 1700, a fort had been erected on the Mississippi River about halfway between Lake Pontchartrain and the Gulf, but the place chosen was most unsuitable, frequently under water and swarming with mosquitoes. It was quickly abandoned. Iberville returned to France in 1702, at the beginning of Queen Anne's War, and was given a naval command. He distinguished himself once more, but in July of 1706, he died of fever in his ship's cabin, barely forty-five years old.

If Iberville was the founder of the Louisiana colony, his brother the Sieur de Bienville was its preserver. In retrospect, it is amazing that Bienville was able to keep the venture alive. Most of the settlers hoped to become rich through mining or the fur trade; none wanted the toilsome life of a farmer, so the crops needed to prevent starvation were not planted. That omission is understandable, because the soil of the Mississippi and Alabama Gulf Coast was so infertile that it returned little for effort expended. The Indians were hostile as often as they were friendly.

Diseases, especially malaria and dysentery, abounded. The number of men in the colony far exceeded the number of women. Under those circumstances, when survival would seem to depend upon co-operation, the colonists constantly quarrelled among themselves, one group supporting Bienville, another opposing him. The French government had been far from successful at managing a colony, and the idea of turning the responsibility over to someone else had obvious appeal. Therefore Louisiana became a proprietary colony.

Antoine Crozat, Marquis de Chatel, was a man who had risen from peasant origins to great wealth and a title of nobility, the latter probably owing to the fact that he was one of the king's creditors. Crozat had made much of his fortune in the slave trade, and he hoped to combine this activity with his Louisiana proprietorship for increased profit. In 1712, when he assumed control of Louisiana, he accepted Antoine de la Mothe Cadillac, already named to the post by Pontchartrain, to govern his new property. Cadillac had come to Canada as an army officer, had prospered after leaving the service, and had founded Detroit. Also, apparently, he had quarrelled with everyone in Canada with whom he had had dealings. Removal to the warmer Louisiana climate did not improve his disposition. His disputatious nature brought him into conflict with almost everyone, but he especially resented Bienville, who had remained in Louisiana as the king's lieutenant, and Jean Baptiste du Bois Duclos, the Commissary. After four years, with hardly a friend left in Louisiana, Cadillac was recalled.

Bienville again served as governor until Jean Michiele, Seigneur de Lépinay, arrived in 1717. The new executive was immediately plunged into the midst of the squabbling that had beset Cadillac, but he did not have to bear with it so long. Back in France Crozat, having spent a fortune with no return in sight, petitioned his government to release him from his proprietorship; and soon after Louisiana was once more in Bienville's hands. Crozat had not done great things for his colony. The population at the beginning of his proprietorship was about four hundred; at the end it was about seven hundred.

It would not be correct, however, to say that nothing at all was accomplished under the first proprietor. Cadillac had brought twenty-five marriageable women with him, and although they were far from being the fairest flowers of France, they brought some contentment to men of the colony. Cadillac also established forts on the Tombigbee River and where the Coosa and Talapoosa come together to form the Alabama; the forts did not halt trade between South Carolina and the Indians along the Mississippi, but they did make it more dangerous for the traders.

Even as the English were a threat from the east, the Spaniards intruded from the west. Juchereau de St. Denis, a young man whose name looms large in Louisiana history, was sent up the Red River to deal with this threat and, if possible, to open trade with Spanish Mexico. The young adventurer established a fort on the Red River in 1714, below a huge log jam that impeded progress farther upstream. The post took its name from the Natchitoches Indians, who welcomed the French, and was the first permanent French settlement on the soil of present-day Louisiana. Action had not been taken too soon; the Spaniards were already at Robeline, only sixteen miles away.

As soon as he felt that it was safe for him to leave the new settlement, St. Denis loaded a pack train with trade goods and set out westward. At San Juan Bautista, on the Rio Grande, he was arrested by the Spanish commandant. For a time he was imprisoned in Mexico City, and Spanish authorities offered him a commission in their army. St. Denis refused and in time was sent back to San Juan Bautista. He must not have been confined very closely, because he managed to woo and win the granddaughter of the commandant, who eventually gave consent to the match. With his bride, St. Denis returned to Natchitoches, where he served as commandant until his death in 1744.

The proprietorship of Louisiana, so happily given up by Crozat in 1717, was eagerly assumed by John Law's Company of the West, soon to become the Company of the Indies. Law was a Scot, apparently a professional gambler, who had hurriedly left his homeland after killing a man in a duel. He conceived the notion of a state bank that would issue notes secured by anticipated government revenues. He was able to persuade the regents of young Louis XV to accept his proposal, and Law became head of the kind of bank he had envisioned. He looked upon Louisiana as a good field for investment, so he organized the Company of the West and in 1717 persuaded the king's ministers to grant Louisiana to the company. In the beginning, there was a mania for speculation in the company's stock, but this "Mississippi Bubble" burst in 1720, and Law had to leave France. His organization—now called the Company of the Indies—continued to administer Louisiana, however, until 1731, when, after fourteen profitless years, it too admitted defeat.

The establishment of New Orleans was probably the most important accomplishment of the Company of the Indies. Bienville had long wanted to build a town where Lake Pontchartrain and the Mississippi River came close together. In 1717 he was instructed to begin construction of a post on the Mississippi, and by the time supplementary instructions designated the junction of Bayou Manchac and the river as the site, Bienville had begun work where New Orleans is today. Despite a hurricane in 1719 that almost necessitated starting over, and despite a recommendation by the company's engineer that a new spot be chosen, Bienville persisted. Another engineer, Adrien de Pauger, drew up the plans for a town that in time became the Vieux Carré of today. The damage done by a second hurricane in 1721 was quickly repaired, because already the town had demonstrated its commercial possibilities. A head count in 1721 showed that almost four hundred people were living in the little village named for the Duke of Orleans. From that time on, New Orleans was the nerve center of colonial Louisiana.

In taking over Louisiana, the company had agreed to transport six thousand colonists and three thousand African slaves a year to its new possession. It never achieved this goal, but it did make an effort. Very few men and women would voluntarily leave France, so some form of coercion was necessary. First, a co-operative French government ordered the release from prison of convicts who would volunteer to go to Louisiana. Most preferred prison in France to freedom in America. The next step was to transport convicts, whether or not they wished to go, and to sweep the streets and highroads of France clean of vagrants, beggars, prostitutes, and almost anyone else who had the bad fortune to fall into the hands of the company's agents. Records show that half the women sent to Louisiana from 1717 to 1721 were prostitutes. The company was dealing with the dregs of French society, and it did not deal gently. The wretched emigrants died like flies at the collection camps in France, and the death rate on the voyage across the Atlantic was as great as or greater than the mortality among slaves making the infamous Middle Passage. Many who survived the voyage were so weakened that they lived only a short time after being put ashore.

Such a policy for colonizing did harm not only to the suffering wretches who were transported; it also harmed Louisiana by introducing people who were as poor material for frontier life as could be found. Very few had any agricultural experience, and most of them had no desire to do any work at all. Instead of cultivating the soil and producing food to feed themselves, they gathered in the wretched little towns, especially New Orleans, and insofar as possible continued the type of life that they had lived in France. As they drank, gambled, and idled their time away, it was necessary to import from France, the West Indies, and the grain-growing settlements of the Illinois country much of the food that kept them alive.

When it became apparent that the type of immigrant thus brought in would not make Louisiana prosper, the company's officials tried another approach. Large grants were offered to men who agreed to provide tenants to work their "concessions." That system had been partially successful in Canada a century earlier, but in Louisiana it availed little. Tenants could not be had from eighteenth-century France. The few concessionaires able to obtain African slaves to work their lands prospered, but it was quickly evident that that was not the way to make Louisiana grow.

A partial solution was found when the company began to seek settlers from outside France. Probably that was the most important contribution that the Company of the Indies made. Louisiana needed farmers, and the company proposed to provide settlers with land, work animals, tools, and enough food to last until the first harvest came in. Germany was still suffering from the aftereffects of the wars of Louis XIV, and many peasants from the Rhineland and from the German-speaking cantons of Switzerland were happy to take advantage of an opportunity to seek greener pastures.

These German settlers suffered also in crossing the Atlantic and becoming accustomed to Louisiana's climate, and sometimes the company would not, or could not, keep its promises about supplies. But that did not halt the migration. No count was made of the number of Germans who came, but so many settled along the Mississippi north of New Orleans, roughly in the area now comprising St. John the Baptist Parish, that that region came to be called the German Coast. Others settled on Bayou Lafourche and in even more remote regions. West of New Orleans, the names Bayou des Allemands and Lake des Allemands give testimony of these early settlers.

The Germans had been hard-working peasants in Europe, and when they came to Louisiana they continued to work, clearing and planting the rich alluvial lands of South Louisiana. In time a few went into the marsh and became hunters and fishermen, but most continued to till the land. They did not add enough to Louisiana's food production to make the colony self-sufficient, but they greatly lessened its dependence upon outside sources. They were exactly the kind of settlers that the colony needed.

Hard work helped the economy, but it did not preserve the German cultural heritage. Within a few generations, the Germans had become almost totally Gallicized. They forgot their native tongue and began to speak French. Harsh Teutonic names were softened into French versions; such common South Louisiana names of today as Triche, Folse, Himel, and Toups are Germanic in origin. A remarkable characteristic of colonial Louisiana was the ability of the French to impose their language and culture upon other nationalities who settled there.

Among those Gallicized were slaves from Africa. The Company of the Indies had agreed to import 3,000 slaves a year, but that was another goal that proved impossible of attainment. How many Africans, or slaves from the West Indies, were imported cannot be determined with any certainty. One ship landed 500 in 1719, and in 1723 another reached New Orleans with 475 hapless Negroes aboard. There were about 2,000 blacks in the colony in 1744, but that may have been fewer than there had been ten years earlier. Negroes were greatly desired. One basic economic weakness of the colony was a shortage of labor, and slaves were a preferred means of relieving that shortage. The demand for more and more agricultural laborers in Louisiana continued long after slavery had come to an end.

The landholders who so eagerly acquired slaves had no idea that they were building an institution that would lead to tragedy, but slavery posed problems almost from the beginning. In 1724, Bienville promulgated the *Code Noir,* a set of laws regulating slaves and the few free Negroes who were by then present in the colony. By today's standards, the *Code Noir* seems barbarously cruel, but in the context of its own time it was actually rather lenient. It was the basis of Louisiana slave law until the late 1820s, when the state adopted parts of the much more severe slave codes of the southeastern states. If slavery was to exist, strict laws were necessary. An insurrection conspiracy was discovered in 1730, resulting in the hanging of one woman and the death after torture of eight men. The fear of black insurrection became so deeply implanted that it would persist for years after slavery had ended.

In 1716, before the founding of New Orleans, Bienville had built Fort Rosalie among the Natchez Indians who lived where the city that bears their name is found today. The original purpose of the station was to reduce British influence among the Indians, but the land at Natchez was fertile, and by 1729 about three hundred French settlers had established themselves there. A Captain Chepart was made commandant of Fort Rosalie, and if the man had deliberately set out to stir up trouble with the Indians, he could not have done much more than he did. Eventually he demanded that the Natchez give up one of their villages so it could be taken over by French settlers. That was the final straw, and the Natchez proceeded to slaughter all but a few of the French at Fort Rosalie.

When the few men who had been fortunate enough to escape the Indians reached New Orleans, Governor Étienne de Périer raised a force of regular soldiers, militia, and Choctaw Indians for a campaign against the Natchez. The tribesmen occupied the French-built fortifications and stoutly resisted siege operations for three weeks in February 1730. Their losses were light, and they easily escaped across the Mississippi, where they continued to make war. It was not until December of 1730 that Périer was able to locate the Natchez at their new encampment in North Louisiana. There, after sporadic fighting, the enemy chieftain, known as "The Sun," was captured and enslaved, as were several hundred women and children and some warriors. Hundreds of fighting men remained free, however, and they sought revenge in a savage attack upon Natchitoches. The indomitable St. Denis drove them away, and thereafter disease and attacks by other Indians rapidly reduced their strength. Most of the few survivors took refuge with their traditional allies, the Chickasaw, but some fled as far east as the Cherokee country in northern Georgia. As a tribe, the Natchez ceased to exist.

In 1731, its resources exhausted, the Company of the Indies begged the French crown to take Louisiana off its hands. The government agreed, and once more Louisiana became a royal colony. Bienville, who had already served as governor three times, and who more than any other man was responsible for the colony's continued existence, was named governor for a fourth term. This time, he would serve for a dozen years, finally to be relieved at his own request so that he might spend his last days in France. It would really not be true to say that Bienville was an inspired administrator; he was not above the petty quarreling that went on almost constantly in French Louisiana, and he was like others in using his official position to line his own pockets. On the other hand, he was superb at averting disaster, and he was at least aware of the real economic needs of the colony. When compared to most other French governors, he stands out.

During his last term as governor, Bienville sought to punish the Chickasaws for the aid they had given the defeated Natchez in 1730. He ordered the Chickasaws to turn over to the French those Natchez who had gone to them as refugees. The warlike nation refused, and Bienville began planning a campaign against them. The plan envisioned a co-ordinated attack by one force

from the Illinois country and another from Mobile under Bienville. As might be expected, the men from the north, moving
downstream by water, arrived first; when Bienville did not appear, they foolishly decided to attack without waiting. The
Chickasaws, advised by traders from the British colonies, were
well prepared. They had dug firing pits under the cabins in their
village, and when the French attacked, they were ready. Those
French who were not killed were captured, and most of the prisoners were tortured to death.

When Bienville finally arrived, he realized his plan had mis-
carried, but he decided to go ahead and attack with his own
force. Once more the Chickasaw were victorious, killing some
thirty of Bienville's troops. He was forced to retreat so hurriedly
that he could not recover the bodies of his dead. The Indians
were clearly the winners in that campaign, and they continued
to wage sporadic warfare against the French for years afterward.
At one time they raided well south of Baton Rouge, and settlers
of the German Coast had to flee from their homes. It was not
until 1752 that the French effected a more or less lasting peace
with the Chickasaw, and by that time France's ownership of
Louisiana had only ten years to run.

Bienville, grown old in the king's service, returned to France
in 1743, leaving Louisiana in the hands of Pierre Rigaud, Marquis de Vaudreuil. Vaudreuil ruled until he was promoted to the
governorship of Canada. He is credited with giving a façade of
continental polish to New Orleans society. No doubt that is true,
but one should not envision in Louisiana a smaller Versailles.
New Orleans was basically a French version of a frontier town,
and the finest food, wine, dress, music, and society available
could not have been very good. A census in 1744 showed a
decline in population since 1731, leaving three thousand white
civilians, eight hundred soldiers, two thousand slaves, and a
few free Negroes. Vaudreuil's successor was Louis Billouart,
Chevalier de Kerlérec, perhaps the most able of French administrators, with the possible exception of Bienville. Kerlérec presided over a colony in which his government had lost interest,
however, and his abilities were largely wasted. The last eighteen years of French control did not bring much growth. When

Spain occupied the colony in 1766, the population may have been as much as seventy-five hundred people of all sorts.

Life in colonial Louisiana was usually short. The subtropical climate encouraged malaria and yellow fever, and the abundance of water provided endless breeding places for the mosquitoes that transmitted these maladies. In addition, almost a third of the people lived in New Orleans, which lacked any effective system of drainage and where the only sewers, if any, were ditches alongside the streets. The streets, innocent of pavement, were six inches deep in dust in dry weather, twelve inches deep in mud in wet. No real concept of sanitation existed, and the practice of medicine in the eighteenth century was so primitive that when one became ill, he was more likely to recover without medical attendance than with it. Conditions in the country were really no better, except that not so many people were crowded together.

Perhaps intimations of mortality strengthened the love of colonial Louisianians for recreation. Hunting and fishing, of course, provided food as well as sport. All classes danced, including slaves who gathered in a certain square of the city for their dances. Christmas was a season of celebration, and the beginnings of the Mardi Gras carnival can be traced back to the French colonial period. Gambling was certainly not unknown in New Orleans, and so many taverns, or saloons, were opened that an attempt was made to restrict their number—an attempt no more successful than subsequent efforts to make New Orleans less hedonistic and more puritanical.

Most of the few attempts to establish schools in French Louisiana quickly failed. An outstanding exception was a school for girls begun by twelve Ursuline nuns in 1727. The nuns taught black and Indian girls as well as white. Boys whose parents could read and write usually did not grow up completely illiterate. They were given the rudiments of an education by their parents or sometimes, in the case of well-to-do families, by a hired tutor. A few men who could afford it sent their sons to France for education. But in general education had the low place in public esteem that might be expected in a frontier community.

The people of French Louisiana were all at least nominally Catholic in religion, but the records make it obvious that many were far from devout. The clergy did not always set the best possible example—in part, because the church in Louisiana was under the Bishop of Quebec, and he was too far away to give adequate supervision. The clergy also lost respect because the Capuchin and Jesuit orders quarrelled bitterly over jurisdictional matters, especially control of the Ursulines. The Capuchins were finally victorious by default, when the Jesuits, who had come into disrepute in Europe, were banned from the colony. Probably most people who lived near a church attended mass, but a sizable number went to church only to be baptized, to be married, and possibly to be buried.

Louisiana never prospered under French rule. Indeed, the colony never became self-sufficient in food production. Corn was the main item in the colonial diet, but the French never learned to like corn, whether green from the fields, ground into meal and boiled in a *gru,* or made into cornbread. They much preferred flour, brought at great expense from the mother country, shipped downriver from the Illinois country, or smuggled in by a trader from the eastern seaboard. Game and fish provided some meat, but most of the pork and beef consumed seems to have come downriver also. In season such vegetables as peas, beans, eggplant, squash, pumpkin, and potatoes might be available. Being French, the people of French Louisiana no doubt made what they had as appetizing as possible, but much of the time the ordinary housewife had very little to work with.

Even if the population had been greater, the colony probably could not have prospered under French rule because it yielded no products for which France provided a good market. Tobacco and indigo were grown and exported, but the types produced in Louisiana were inferior to those produced in the West Indies and therefore brought low prices. Since the colony had little to sell, it had an unfavorable balance of trade, which meant that the people had difficulty in paying for imported necessities. In practice, most imports were paid for with drafts on the French government, which was an attempt to draw water from an almost-dry well: from the time of Louis XIV onward, the

French treasury was on the verge of bankruptcy. After bankrupting Antoine Crozat, John Law, and the Company of the Indies, Louisiana imposed an annual burden of perhaps $1.5 million upon the French government, and there was no indication of any early improvement.

France was never over-interested in Louisiana. Proprietorship of the colony was given first to Crozat, then to John Law; after it again became a royal colony it was neglected. Officials sent to Louisiana were probably no more incompetent, venal, and quarrelsome than those named to office in France, but they certainly were largely incompetent, venal, and quarrelsome, and Louisiana was not as able as France to withstand such administration. Probably the origin of chronic corruption in Louisiana government can be traced to the French attitude that office was a form of property from which the holder should profit. Obviously, Louisiana was not a possession that France would make sacrifices to keep; on the contrary, the colony was a burden that the king's government might seek to place upon the shoulders of another power.

2

A Holding Action: Louisiana
as a Spanish Colony

PAIN was the power fortunate—or unfortunate—enough to obtain Louisiana from France. Spanish administration was far more successful than French administration had been, but the success of Spanish Louisiana was comparative, not absolute. The colony continued to be an economic burden, but its primary purpose in the minds of Spanish officials was strategic, not economic.

In 1754 the French and Indian War broke out in the backwoods of Pennsylvania; by 1756 hostilities between France and Britain had spread to Europe. Louisiana's role in the conflict was minimal; the main effect upon the colony was that trade was cut off between New Orleans and Europe. France won victories in the early fighting, but soon her army and navy fell upon hard times, and one British victory followed another. In 1761 Spain foolishly honored the "Family Compact" between the two Bourbon powers and became France's ally. Spain's belligerency did not have any significant effect upon the course of the war, and the British fleet quickly deprived her of Havana and Manila. In 1762, by the Treaty of Fontainebleau, France ceded Louisiana to Spain. It was almost certain that Spain would lose Florida to England in the peace settlement, and the cession of Louisiana may have been partly to compensate Spain for that loss. A more important motivation, however, was simply to be rid of Louisiana and its never-ceasing demands upon the French treasury. In 1763, a general peace was effected by the Treaty of Paris of that year. France gave up Canada, gave up her claims to lands south of the Great Lakes and east of the Mississippi, and ceded to England all of the territory claimed by France east of the Mississippi except the "Isle of Orleans," set off by Bayou Manchac, the Amite River, and Lakes Maurepas, Pontchartrain, and Borgne. Thus New Orleans remained part of Louisiana. The ceded portion east of the Mississippi became part of British West Florida.

Spain's rulers were not ignorant of the condition of Louisiana, nor did they have any illusions about making the province profitable. They were concerned about the fact that the peace settlement put the British on the east bank of the Mississippi River, far nearer to the truly valuable Spanish colonies to the west than they had been before the war. At the very least, Louisiana provided space as a defense against a British move toward Mexico and New Mexico from the north or east. At the best, it offered a springboard for a counterattack, and in fact it would serve that purpose during the American Revolution and enable the Spaniards to recover Florida, though only temporarily.

Spain was in no hurry to take physical possession of her new colony. Governor Kerlérec was recalled to France in the spring of 1763, and Jean Jacques Blaise d'Abbadie was left in charge. It was not until late 1764 that d'Abbadie received official notification of Louisiana's cession to Spain, including orders to turn the colony over to Spanish officials when they should arrive. But months passed, and no Spanish officials arrived; furthermore, when the people of the colony were informed of the cession, they refused to accept it. The French flag continued to fly over New Orleans, and a prominent citizen, Jean Milhet, went to France and enlisted the aid of the aged Bienville in an attempt to bring about a change in policy. Louis XV refused even to give an audience, and the king's minister, the Duke de Choiseul, refused to be influenced.

D'Abbadie died in early 1765 and was succeeded by Charles

Philippe Aubry, a man whose reputation has suffered at the hands of some traditional Louisiana historians. In fact, Aubry seems to have obeyed instructions from the French government so long as he held office. Late in the summer he received a message from Don Antonio de Ulloa, announcing that Ulloa had been selected to take possession of Louisiana in the name of Spain, but more months passed, and Ulloa did not arrive. Small wonder that some of the colonists almost forgot about the change in sovereignty, or that some of them began to hope that it would not really take place.

Ulloa finally landed in New Orleans in March of 1766. His small entourage included only eighty soldiers, enough, perhaps, to antagonize the population, but not enough to control it. Ulloa was one of the leading scholars of his age, much respected in Europe, but he apparently had little gift for colonial administration. It should be noted that his instructions were that Louisiana should not be governed as the rest of the Spanish Empire was, and that no change in its existing government should be made. That, presumably, is why Ulloa left Aubry and the Superior Council in charge of administration while he made a thorough tour inspecting the colony.

More than a dozen prominent men of New Orleans had apparently been consulting together since before Ulloa's arrival. Some of them had economic interests at stake. Also involved was the Superior Council, which had gradually assumed administrative responsibilities, although it had been created to serve as a judicial body. Under d'Abbadie and Aubry, it had a very large, perhaps decisive, role in the government of the colony. Its power could be lost under Spanish administrations. On the other hand, Louisiana being Louisiana, perhaps the arrival from Spain of a new regulation prohibiting the importation of any but Spanish wines was the last straw. At any rate, the guns at the gates of New Orleans were spiked on the night of October 27, and the next day a gathering of some four hundred persons dominated by a group of merchants demanded expulsion of the Spanish. Ulloa left his home in the city and set up headquarters on a ship in the river. On the twenty-ninth, a mob again demonstrated, and after it had dispersed, the Superior Council ordered

Ulloa and his troops to leave Louisiana. Aubry had protested against this illegal action, but he did nothing else to prevent it, and Ulloa went downstream to Balize from whence he sailed to Cuba on November 16, 1768.

Early historians of Louisiana depicted the insurrection of 1768 as a blow for freedom and compared it with the revolution that soon began in the British colonies. There are some resemblances, in that the insurrection was directed by a relatively few men, some of them with economic considerations in mind, but that is about as far as the similarities go. The Louisiana rebels had no idea of self-government; the mob, to the extent that it was not merely having a drunken good time, hoped for French rather than Spanish autocracy. Furthermore, the little Louisiana colony had no chance of achieving anything by revolt; it was as if Georgia alone had rebelled against British rule in 1775.

For less than a year, Aubry presided over a colony that, at least at the center, was deluded into believing that it had successfully defied the power of Spain. Aubry himself wrote letters to both France and to Cuba, seeking to protect himself, whatever the outcome might be. In this he was wise, for in August 1769, a Spanish fleet of twenty-four ships carrying two thousand troops and General Alejandro O'Reilly anchored at New Orleans. O'Reilly was of Irish birth; he had fled to Spain to avoid the persecution of Catholics in Ireland, entered the Spanish army, and demonstrated great ability. In 1765 he had saved the life of King Charles III during a riot in Madrid. A lieutenant general in 1769, O'Reilly was not a scholar like Ulloa, but rather a superb administrator who knew how to use force effectively.

In addition to orders making him captain general and governor, O'Reilly had specific instructions to punish the leaders of the rebellion against Ulloa. Aubry, under orders from France to co-operate, named the instigators, a dozen of whom were arrested on the morning of August 21. Two days later amnesty was granted to all other participants in the rebellion, but the people were ordered to take an oath of allegiance to the king of Spain. The conspirators received full due process under Spanish law, but they were obviously guilty and were so found. One of them died in prison. Five others were sentenced to death and shot; the remaining six were sent to prison in Havana and suffered confiscation of their property. For O'Reilly to have done any less than he did would have been to encourage another rebellion. He had legal grounds for action against other participants, but he limited punishment to the twelve ringleaders. French-speaking historians wrote the first accounts of the affair, however, and "bloody O'Reilly" became a villian in the schoolbooks. Later historians have, however, treated him more kindly.

O'Reilly was in Louisiana only seven months, but the reassertion of Spanish authority and the punishment of the rebels were only a small part of his accomplishments. The man was a whirlwind of energy and a most able administrator. He sent representatives throughout the colony to report on conditions, and he personally went up the Mississippi as far as Pointe Coupee. A census was taken, showing some 13,500 people in the colony, a rapid increase probably brought about by the Acadian migration. New Orleans had more than 3,000 people. Spanish law was substituted for French law, and an abridged version was published in French. The Superior Council was abolished, but in New Orleans the *Cabildo,* or town council, was created to replace it, and O'Reilly ordered that a suitable building be erected for the *Cabildo's* deliberations. The general found time for a council with the Indians, staging a sham battle to show the power of Spain. Probably nothing demonstrated his judgment more, however, than the fact that he quickly began returning the troops he brought with him to Cuba and organized a Louisiana militia of about 1,000 men. He put Spanish laws regulating trade into force, but looked the other way while trade essential to the colony's existence went on with the British. Indeed, O'Reilly himself purchased a shipload of flour from Oliver Pollock, an American merchant whom he had met earlier in Havana. O'Reilly left Louisiana definitely under Spanish control, and the successor whom he designated, Don Luis de Unzaga, enjoyed a relatively placid administration.

Spanish political administration of Louisiana was far more detailed than French, but it differed from that of other Spanish colonies. The governor was chief executive and, in general, had the last word on all but religious matters. An intendant was responsible for revenues and in charge of commercial matters in general. Lieutenant governors presided over the distant posts of Natchez and St. Louis, each at the site of the present city of the same name. For local administration, the colony was divided into districts, each under a commandant. The districts were in turn subdivided into areas supervised by an official known as the *syndic*.

The administration of justice began with the *syndic*, at the local level. More serious cases were heard by the commandant of the district, who was as much a civil and judicial officer as a military one. In New Orleans the *Cabildo* was divided into a number of courts for different types of cases, and it took cases on appeal from the commandants. Early in the Spanish period, the *Cabildo* was the court of last resort, but later it became possible to appeal a case involving larger amounts of money to Havana and even to Spain. Criminal law was far removed from British or American practice, inasmuch as the accused was given no opportunity to face his accusers or to cross-examine witnesses, but a reading of abstracts of hearings leaves the impression that the court normally arrived at the truth. Punishments were sometimes barbarous, but no more so than those prescribed by British law at the same time.

O'Reilly had divided Louisiana into twenty-one parishes and placed it under the jurisdiction of the Bishop of Santiago de Cuba rather than the Bishop of Quebec. O'Reilly's parishes were purely ecclesiastical, but they were later to become the basis for political subdivision. In 1790 the churches of Louisiana were put within the diocese of the Bishop of Havana. Finally, in 1795, Louisiana and Florida became a diocese under Bishop Luis Ignacio Penalver. Rivalry between French and Spanish Capuchins and probably some resentment of Spanish domination by the French-speaking population seems to have led to considerable anticlericalism, especially in New Orleans. The ideas of the French Revolution no doubt played a part in this also. Country people were more often devout, but there were simply not enough priests and churches to serve such a widely scattered population. Bishop Penalver was especially disturbed by the coming of Protestants into his diocese. "The emigration from the western part of the United States and the toleration of our government," he wrote, "have introduced into this colony a gang of adventurers who have no religion and acknowledge no God. . . . It is true that the same resistance to religion has always manifested itself here, but never with such scandal as now prevails." [1] In July of 1801 Penalver was made Archbishop of Guatemala, and Louisiana was left once more without a resident head of the church.

Probably the most striking feature of the Spanish period in Louisiana history is the tremendous increase in population. There were perhaps seventy-five hundred people in the colony in 1763; by 1803 the number had grown to approximately fifty thousand. Although such a rate of growth is not comparable to that of Massachusetts Bay between 1630 and 1640, it is certainly comparable to most of the British North American colonies. Most of the growth in population came through immigration, which generous land policies did much to encourage. Heads of families were entitled to 350 to 475 yards of frontage along a river or bayou, as well as seed, tools, and a year's provisions. Land tracts extended back from a stream as much as 40 arpents, or roughly one and one-half miles. In South Louisiana, however, the land slopes downward away from the streams, and ordinarily the ground had become too low to cultivate long before that distance from the waterfront was reached. Because the streams did not run in straight lines, but rather in loops and curves, lines drawn back from the water led to strangely shaped landholdings. To this day, land plats of the longer-settled portions of Southern Louisiana show narrow strips, pie-shaped tracts, and wedge-shaped blocks fronting the streams, while back in the swamps are the regular, square sections of the United States land survey according to the Land Ordinance of 1785.

Acadians were the most numerous immigrants. They were the

1. Charles Gayarré, *History of Louisiana,* 4 vols. (1903; reprint ed., New Orleans: Pelican Publishing Company, 1965), 3:407–408.

descendants of French emigrants who had settled in Nova Scotia, then called Acadia, in the seventeenth century. In 1713, at the end of the War of the Spanish Succession, France had ceded Nova Scotia to Great Britain. The people, as might have been expected, remained loyal to France, and when the War of the Austrian Succession (King George's War) began, British authorities decided that it was necessary to deport several thousand Acadians. As many more fled from their homes without waiting for deportation. Many went to Canada, many back to France, and quite a number to the British colonies on the English seaboard. In Canada these people seem to have felt more or less at home and to have adapted to the situation. Those who went to France, however, and especially those who went to the English colonies, were not happy and were ready to move on elsewhere. With the end of the Seven Years War in 1763, they began taking advantage of the generous land grants available in Louisiana. There is some dispute over how many came to the colony, with estimates ranging from less than five thousand to more than ten thousand, though the smaller figure seems somewhat improbable.

The first Acadians settled in the Attakapas region, centering more or less about modern St. Martinville, but subsequent groups took up lands along Bayou Lafourche and on the Mississippi, where two areas well south of Baton Rouge became known as the Acadian Coasts. They were superb colonists for Louisiana—simple, hardworking, deeply religious, asking only to be let alone. To this day they make up an important element of the population, and they have expanded eastward into southern Mississippi and Alabama and westward into Texas. Some of them quickly merged into the mainstream of Louisiana life. Others, particularly those in isolated areas, tended to maintain an almost completely separate society. As late as the 1950s, driving an automobile in South Central Louisiana on Sunday was made difficult by the horses and buggies of "Cajun" families going to and returning from mass. Even today there is a Cajun dialect, Cajun music, and Cajun cooking, each a thing to be prized. Indeed it is possible in 1976 to find in Louisiana grandparents whose only language is French.

Next to Acadians, people from the British colonies or, later, the United States, probably were the second largest group of immigrants. The Spanish authorities granted freedom of conscience to Protestant immigrants, although no public worship other than Catholic was permitted. Most Americans came as individuals or as families, but some settled on large grants. American migration gathered momentum during the Revolutionary War, and it continued afterward. The presence of English-speaking people, and even communities, in Louisiana and West Florida helped to make Americanization simpler after the Louisiana Purchase.

Relatively few people from Spain settled in Louisiana. A group of Canary Islanders settled along lower Bayou Lafourche and north of Lake Maurepas, but they were not numerous enough to influence Louisiana culture significantly. Likewise a group of settlers from Malaga, in Spain, were led by one Francisco Bouligny to the lower Teche and established New Iberia. Adding to the increase of population were French Santo Domingans who fled the insurrection there and came to Louisiana. People from France, Germany, and other continental European nations also sought in Louisiana better opportunities than they had found at home.

The black population increased almost as rapidly as the white. During the last years of the French regime the number of Africans imported had declined, but under Spain there was a strong revival of the traffic in human beings. Plantation agriculture had definitely made a beginning by the 1790s, although the cultivation of cotton and sugar on a large scale did not begin until late in the decade. Probably as many slaves came from the West Indies, especially Santo Domingo, as from Africa, until the Santo Domingo insurrection began, after which the Spanish government restricted the trade severely. Smuggling went on on a fairly significant scale; waterways afforded so many means of access to Louisiana that it was almost impossible to prevent smuggling of Negroes so long as people desired to buy them.

Emancipation of slaves had been relatively easy under French law, and that continued to be true under Spain. By 1803 there were an estimated thirteen hundred free black people in New

Orleans and a few others elsewhere in the colony. Some of them had been free when they arrived from Santo Domingo; some were even slaveowners, and the more able and enterprising among them were accumulating wealth. Much has been written of the custom of *placage,* according to which young white men, until they married, took free Negro girls as mistresses and sometimes maintained them afterward. That practice certainly did exist; and although it was practiced by a definite minority of young white men and a definite minority of young free black women, to the extent that it was practiced, it resulted in constantly increasing dilution of African blood among the free people of color.

Certainly by the end of the colonial period the people of Louisiana were made up of many strains. From the darkest African to the lightest Caucasian, from the northern European German to the Latin from southern Europe, the people of the colony were indeed a mixed group. Josiah Quincy of Massachusetts was not inaccurate in his descriptions when he objected to the admission of Louisiana to the Union on the grounds that Congress had no right to extend the rights of United States citizens to "a *hotch-pot* with the wild men on the Missouri, nor with the mixed, though more respectable race of Anglo-Hispanic-Gallo-Americans who bask on the sands at the mouth of the Mississippi." [2] Quincy's was a lost cause, and the "mixed though more respectable race" would come into the Union as citizens of a state and would make a distinctive contribution to the American melting pot before the term had ever been used.

As compared with the conditions of things under French administration, Louisiana prospered under Spanish rule. Money remained scarce, but enough Spanish silver circulated to afford an effective means of exchange. Spain's trade regulations would have stifled the colony had they been strictly enforced, but Louisiana was always a special case in the eyes of Spanish administrators, and Spanish officials learned through necessity that they must sometimes ignore the smugglers whose illegal activi-

2. Gayarré, *History of Louisiana,* 4:257.

ties kept the colony alive. Spanish officials, who had the same attitude toward profiting from office as their French predecessors, got their share of the returns from smuggling. Trade with France, permitted under special conditions, was extensive, and by the end of the colonial period most trade was with the United States.

Much of that trade came down the Mississippi, especially after the Pinckney Treaty of 1795 gave western Americans the right of deposit at New Orleans. Ships bearing exports away from New Orleans were more likely to be under the flag of the United States than under that of any other nation. They carried mainly tobacco, deer hides, salt meat, flour, and some indigo. They brought flour from the middle states, manufactured goods from Europe, and such luxuries as coffee, tile, soap, textiles, and shoes. One-third of all imports by weight was made up of alcoholic beverages, and since these liquors were shipped in barrels, it was necessary to import many bottles for the use of retail establishments. In the 1790s, near the end of the Spanish period, the development of the cotton gin made cotton into a major crop, and in 1796 Étienne de Boré developed a process for making sugar from cane grown in Louisiana. Cotton and sugar soon became Louisiana's two major money crops. Though Louisiana was much more prosperous under Spain than she had been under France, the colony was yet an economic liability, costing Spain perhaps $500,000 a year.

Spain legally possessed Louisiana from 1762 until 1800, and she actually controlled the colony from 1769 to 1803. New Iberia and Iberia Parish are testimony to the settlement of Spaniards in Louisiana, and to this day Spanish surnames are encountered. But by and large Spain had little lasting influence. The French language, the French approach to religion, the French attitude toward pleasure, and French dietary habits remained dominant, and when the Spaniards had departed, it was almost as if they had not come. Their chief monuments are physical. The architecture of the Vieux Carré in New Orleans is Spanish, not French, because the city was almost totally destroyed by great fires in 1788 and 1794, and it was rebuilt in Spanish style. There is a certain irony in the fact that New

Orleans, its older section Spanish in architecture, its population mainly black, Irish, Anglo-American, and Italian, is nonetheless thought of as a French city. French culture won almost a total victory over the Spanish; it would encounter a much more formidable adversary in the Anglo-Americans.

3

Louisiana in the American Revolution

$\mathcal{OS}$PANISH Louisiana was far removed from Bunker Hill, Valley Forge, and Yorktown, but the colony did play an important, though little-known, part in the American Revolution. Louisiana's role was not so much in actual warfare, though Governor Bernardo de Gálvez's campaigns deserve attention. The importance of Louisiana's contribution to the cause of the Revolution lay, first, in the strengthening of the American claim to the Old Northwest, and, second, in the effect of Gálvez's victories upon the future expansion of the United States. The years that followed the recognition of American independence saw jockeying between Spain and the new republic for control of present-day Alabama and Mississippi, a diplomatic contest in which the Americans were victorious.

Events leading to the American Revolution corresponded in time with Spain's taking over Louisiana. The Stamp Act was passed the year before Ulloa arrived in New Orleans. Governor O'Reilly, having firmly established Spanish control of the province, left it the year of the Boston Massacre. O'Reilly's appointee, Luis de Unzaga, was governing Louisiana when the first blood was shed at Lexington and Concord. Gálvez became governor in 1777, the year that the American victory at Saratoga persuaded France to ally herself with the revolting British colonies. It was not surprising, then, that the fate of Louisiana and of the English-speaking people on the Atlantic seaboard should be bound together.

A New Orleans merchant named Oliver Pollock was of great importance to the American cause. Pollock was born and grew up in northern Ireland and came to Pennsylvania with his father about 1760. After a period in Havana, where he met O'Reilly, Pollock moved to New Orleans and set up a mercantile business in 1768, the year before O'Reilly's expedition arrived. When the new governor's troops ran short of provisions, Pollock turned over to him, for whatever price O'Reilly chose to pay, a shipload of flour. He had made an excellent investment. O'Reilly had been instructed to halt illegal trade with the British colonies, and he expelled five British merchants from Louisiana. Pollock was allowed to stay.

When the American Revolution began, Spain was in a quandary as to what course to follow. The king of Spain ruled over more colonies than any other monarch in the world, and the encouragement of rebellion was certainly to be avoided. On the other hand, England was Spain's hereditary enemy; England held Gibraltar on the Iberian Peninsula and only a dozen years earlier, at the close of the Seven Years War, had taken Florida from Spain and the area between the Perdido River and the Mississippi from France. British posts at Manchac (between New Orleans and Baton Rouge), Baton Rouge, and Natchez were a direct threat to Spanish Louisiana. Britain's possession of Mobile and Pensacola was a threat to Spanish shipping in the Gulf of Mexico, and the British posts in Florida could, and did to some extent, serve as bases for trade with Spanish colonies in defiance of Spanish trade policy. Later, after France entered the war, Spain's "Family Compact" with France inclined Spain still more to oppose England. Eventually, Spain would go to war, but it was made very clear that she went as an ally of France, not of the United States.

Governor Unzaga had instructions to keep a careful watch over events in North America that might affect Spain, and the Spanish government was willing to extend aid to the colonies secretly. When Captain George Gibson arrived in New Orleans with a letter from General Charles Lee asking for aid, Unzaga sold him ten thousand pounds of gunpowder and accepted a draft on the government of Virginia, endorsed by Pollock. About seventy-five hundred pounds of this powder were carried upriver to what are now Pittsburgh and Wheeling, where it was badly needed for defense against British and Indian attacks. Pollock shipped the remaining twenty-five hundred pounds to Philadelphia by sea. Unzaga informed his successor that if Spain was going to fight against Great Britain, Pollock was the only British merchant in New Orleans who could be trusted. However, he said, if Spain should decide to support Britain, Pollock should not be allowed to remain in New Orleans twenty-four hours.

Gálvez was a younger and more enthusiastic man than Unzaga, and perhaps he would for that reason have been more inclined on his own initiative to aid the Americans in their battle against Britain. However, less than two months after taking office, Gálvez received from his government notification of a shipment of various supplies that he was discreetly to put into the hands of the Americans. Thus, it was official Spanish policy to provide secret aid for the revolutionaries. By the end of Gálvez's first year in office, more than seventy thousand dollars' worth of supplies had been sent from New Orleans to the upper Ohio.

In early 1778 a former resident of Natchez named James Willing, son of a prominent Philadelphian, led an expedition down the Mississippi against West Florida. His instructions have not been preserved, but apparently he had been ordered by the Commerce Committee of the Continental Congress to persuade the people of West Florida, by force if necessary, to support the Revolutionary cause. Also he was expected to capture and/or destroy such British property as he could with his small force of about thirty men, all transported downriver aboard a small boat appropriately named *Rattletrap*. When Willing arrived at Natchez in February 1778, most of the settlement's residents took an oath not to bear arms against the United States or aid the enemies of the United States. Those who did not take the oath and all who had held any sort of office under the British saw their slaves and other moveable property seized, and often their homes were burned.

In New Orleans Willing received protection from Governor Gálvez, but so did refugees who had fled from his attack. It is

difficult to see how Willing's expedition served any useful purpose. Of far more importance to the American cause was aid
given to George Rogers Clark. Western Virginia, including
what is now Kentucky, was constantly harassed by Indians from
north of the Ohio. These Indians were supplied and presumably
incited by British officers stationed in what had been the Illinois
country of French Louisiana, and Clark was commissioned by
Governor Patrick Henry of Virginia to raise troops and move
against the former French posts north of the Ohio. In a brilliant
campaign, no doubt made easier by the fact that the French in
the area had no particular love for the British, Clark captured
Kaskaskia, Cahokia, and Vincennes during the summer of
1778. His achievement was cheered by the Spanish west of the
Mississippi, mainly at St. Louis, in what is now Missouri.

The English were not ready to give up these posts. Colonel
Henry Hamilton, known as "the Hair Buyer" by the people of
the West, massed five hundred British troops, volunteers, and
Indians, and in mid-December recaptured Vincennes from the
small force Clark had left there. Hamilton, believing that winter
now made campaigning impossible, sent his Indians and militia
home and remained at Vincennes with ninety men. Clark gathered seventy Americans and sixty French volunteers and set out
in February 1779 for Vincennes. Their march in the dead of
winter, often through waist-deep flood waters, is justly celebrated. Outside of Vincennes, Clark managed to let the towns-
people know of his arrival while keeping it secret from the British, which says something more about the loyalty of the French
of the Illinois country to the British crown. As every schoolboy
once knew, Clark then proceeded to capture the British garrison, including Colonel Hamilton, who was led in ignominious
captivity through the Kentucky settlements to Virginia.

Clark operated under the authority of the state of Virginia,
but authority was about all the state could give him. The French
people of the Illinois country gave him some help, but most of
the wherewithal for his work came from Pollock and Gálvez.
The ammunition for his original campaign included gunpowder
previously shipped to Fort Pitt from New Orleans, and to keep
control over Indians who might have turned against him, Clark

distributed goods worth $7,200 that reached him from New Orleans in September of 1778. At the same time he received more gunpowder. In addition to relying on actual goods sent from New Orleans, Clark depended upon Pollock's credit for buying supplies locally. Technically, he paid for such goods with drafts on the treasury of the state of Virginia, but in reality the paper had value only because Pollock placed his personal credit behind it.

From the time he took office as governor, Gálvez had sought to strengthen the defenses of Louisiana in general and New Orleans in particular. He realized, however, that he was unlikely to get enough men or material to defend so large an area and made up his mind that in the event of war, which grew more and more likely, he should take the offensive. Spain feared most of all an attack from Canada down the Mississippi; therefore Gálvez planned to move first against Baton Rouge and Natchez. But when he sent his adjutant, one Jacinto Panis, to Mobile and Pensacola on a diplomatic mission, he instructed Panis to observe carefully the fortifications and general military strength of these two posts; Panis did his work well and even drew up a plan for attacking Pensacola that Gálvez followed, with modifications, when the time came.

The Spanish government decided in the spring of 1779 to go to war with England on June 21; the official notice of this decision, plus instructions to capture West Florida, reached Gálvez in early August. He had some 600 troops, but 450 of them were untrained recruits, and many of the remainder were weakened by sickness. Gálvez's own officers, with few exceptions, believed that he was preparing to defend New Orleans, and a council of war recommended surrender in case of attack. In reality he intended from the beginning to go on the offensive and ordered an advance upriver to begin on August 23; but on August 18 a hurricane sank the boats he had collected and did much damage to New Orleans. Driving himself and his men harder than ever, Gálvez set out on August 27, only four days later than he had planned. His force totaled 667 men, of whom 80 were free blacks and 7 were Americans. One of the Americans was Pollock, representing Virginia and the Continental

Congress and serving as Gálvez's aide-de-camp. As this little army marched upriver, it was reinforced by another 600 militiamen from the German Coast and Acadian settlements along the river. Gálvez was greatly outnumbered by the British and their Indian allies in West Florida, but he had more men than his enemies had at any one point; this was essential to the success of his plans.

Manchac fell easily; nearly all the British troops had retreated to Baton Rouge, where for six weeks they had been erecting fortifications. Behind these defenses were four hundred regular troops, one hundred and fifty settlers and armed blacks, and thirteen cannon. Gálvez began a bombardment with his heavier artillery on the morning of September 21, and by mid-afternoon the British were forced to surrender. The terms of the surrender at Baton Rouge included the little garrison at Natchez also. In less than a month, Gálvez had removed any British threat to the navigation of the Mississippi except for occasional sniping by Chickasaw Indians and Tories from the area of present-day Memphis. Farther north, a British and Indian attack on St. Louis failed dismally.

Mobile was Gálvez's next objective, but that would have to be an amphibious operation; no road existed for a march around the lakes and along the Gulf Coast. The governor sought naval support from Havana, but when the commandant there found one reason after another for not sending ships, Gálvez decided to go ahead on his own. He did succeed in getting 560 additional troops from Cuba. Added to the men he already had, the reinforcement gave him a total of more than 1,000 men for the attack on Mobile. On February 10, 1781, he attempted to enter Mobile Bay, but several ships went aground. That misadventure, followed by very bad weather, cost Gálvez some men, some of his artillery, and a sizable amount of supplies, but like the hurricane at New Orleans the previous year, it seems to have infused new energy into his efforts. By March 1 he had landed his troops and brought them up to Mobile, though siege operations had not yet begun. He and the English commander, Captain Elias Durnford, carried on a most courteous correspondence, exchanging gifts of food and wine, and assuring one another of mutual respect, but there was more than a survival of chivalry in this exchange of courtesies. Gálvez needed time to get his artillery in position for siege operations; Durnford, on the other hand, knew that a relief force was on its way overland from Pensacola, so the longer he could delay matters the better his chances for rescue.

On the night of March 9, Gálvez began placing his artillery, and at ten o'clock in the morning, the Spanish guns began firing. At sundown Durnford ran up a white flag, and negotiations for surrender began. Probably Durnford dragged out the negotiations as long as he could, but on March 13 he surrendered. On March 15, a Spanish patrol encountered, only twenty-five miles east of Mobile, the vanguard of eleven hundred men advancing westward from Pensacola. The commander of this force, General John Campbell, turned back to Pensacola when he learned that Mobile had already fallen.

An attack on Pensacola would require substantial reinforcement from Cuba, and despite Gálvez's best efforts, he could not persuade the Cuban authorities to send the necessary help in time to keep the momentum of his offensive. He eventually found it necessary to go himself to Havana, and in October he sailed from there with a formidable fleet and almost four thousand troops. Once more nature seemed determined to thwart him: a hurricane scattered the fleet and made action in 1780 impossible.

By February, Gálvez was ready for another try. This time he got a weaker naval force from Havana, and only 1,315 men, but to them he added men from Mobile and New Orleans. His biggest problem was obtaining the co-operation of the naval commander, who was most reluctant to take his ships into the harbor under long-range fire from British guns in Fort Barrancas, which guarded the harbor entrance. Gálvez was fortunate in that he had one ship, the *Gálveztown*, under his own command. That craft he sailed into the harbor in defiance of the British guns, and without damage. Before doing so he sent a message to the reluctant Captain José Calbo de Branzabal, stating what he was about to do, and pointing out that his reason for doing so was to "remove fear." Calbo followed the next day, though it is difficult to say whether he was most influenced by the reflection on his courage or by the fact that Gálvez had sent him a detailed description of the channel.

Soon after the Spanish fleet entered the harbor, troops from Mobile and New Orleans arrived; on April 19 a new fleet came from Havana, carrying both French and Spanish troops. Including sailors who were sent ashore, these reinforcements gave Gálvez more than seven thousand men to use against sixteen hundred English and Tory troops and their much more numerous Indian allies, including Choctaws, Creeks, Seminoles, and even some Chickasaws. The British concentrated their defense in Fort George, and Indian forays caused most of the Spanish casualties until the very last of April, when actual siege operations began.

Once the siege did begin, the fate of the garrison was sealed, though it put up a spirited resistance. The bombardment went on for more than a week; it might have continued much longer, but on the morning of March 8 a lucky shot from a Spanish howitzer struck the powder magazine of a redoubt guarding the approach to Fort George. The resulting explosion killed perhaps a hundred of the garrison and left the position defenseless. The Spaniards quickly occupied the ruins and brought up guns to fire into the fort at almost point-blank range. British casualties under such fire were heavy, and in mid-afternoon General Campbell asked for an armistice. The formal surrender, which included all of West Florida, took place on May 10, 1781.

After Pensacola, Gálvez was ordered to attack the British island of Jamaica, but the war ended before that campaign could be launched. After a year in Spain, he returned to the New World, in October 1784, loaded with honors. He was Viceroy of New Spain, with control over Cuba and Louisiana as well, and all his titles make a fairly long printed paragraph. He was exceedingly popular in Mexico, but he died in 1786, little more than forty years old.

Louisiana's part in the Revolutionary War probably did not hasten the end of the war. On the other hand, the success of George Rogers Clark's campaign certainly strengthened the claim of the United States to the Old Northwest, and that is true whether or not the negotiators discussed the matter. Of more importance to the future of Louisiana, and probably to the future of the United States, was the fact that Gálvez's campaign resulted in Florida's being ceded to Spain in the peace that followed the Revolution. Canada remained British, and it is not a part of the United States nor likely ever to be. Florida went to Spain; and in less than thirty years, West Florida had been annexed to the United States. In less than forty years, so had the rest of Florida. Eight Louisiana parishes of today, including East Baton Rouge, where the state capital is located, were once part of Florida.

The Treaty of Paris of 1783 gave the United States all lands south of the Great Lakes, east of the Mississippi, and north of a line along the thirty-first parallel of latitude west of the Apalachicola River, down that river to the Flint River, east to the St. Mary's River, and down that stream to the Atlantic. Thus Spanish territory bordered the new nation to the west and to the south. However, the treaty between Great Britain and Spain did not specify what the northern boundary of Florida should be, and Natchez had certainly been administered as part of British West Florida. Spain continued to occupy Natchez after the peace and claimed that Florida extended as far north as the Tennessee River.

Spain's objective in the Revolutionary War, insofar as the Western Hemisphere was concerned, was, as noted, not to help the United States but rather to weaken Great Britain. According to mercantilist theory, loss of the colonies would help serve this purpose. On the other hand, the new United States could be a threat to Spain's North American possessions as great as Great Britain had been, or greater. During the Revolution Americans poured over the mountains into Kentucky and Tennessee, and with peace more came. Once west of the mountains, these settlers were economically at the mercy of whoever held New Orleans, and it was only natural that they should desire to control that city. They would have to wait for actual possession until the Louisiana Purchase of 1803, but in the meantime some enterprising westerners saw a chance to obtain special privileges and welcome payments in money from the Spanish treasury.

The so-called Spanish Conspiracy has attracted much attention from historians of the frontier, but to this day it is impossible to say who was doing what to whom. In 1784 the lower Mississippi was closed to all but Spanish ships. That directive was not stringently enforced, but it caused great concern among western settlers. Their fears were further aroused when a treaty—never ratified—was negotiated that would have closed the lower Mississippi to navigation by Americans for twenty-five years. That did result in some talk among westerners of separation from the United States. Several Kentuckians, led by James Wilkinson, who had been a general in the Revolution, began some sort of negotiations with Spain on their own. Wilkinson went to New Orleans in 1787, took an oath of allegiance to Spain, and began receiving more or less regular payments from the Spanish government.

Wilkinson apparently convinced Louisiana's Governor Esteban Miró and François Louis Hector, Baron de Carondelet, who in 1791 succeeded Miró, that there was a chance that the Southwest would separate from the United States and become an independent republic dependent upon Spain, or even that the people of the Southwest might be willing to become subjects of the king of Spain. At the same time, Wilkinson kept Miró and then Carondelet fearful that the wild men of the West might, on their own, launch an attack upon New Orleans. In return Wilkinson and his friends gained a near monopoly of trade down the Mississippi, and Wilkinson got his pension. It seems today that these gentlemen had no real thought of a western republic or of being annexed by Spain. They were, in a sense, confidence men, taking advantage of the gullibility of the Spaniards, and of Carondelet in particular, to achieve personal advantages and personal fortunes. The Spanish Conspiracy, such as it was, collapsed with the ratification of Pinckney's Treaty in 1795, but Wilkinson remained on the Spanish payroll for years afterward, basically as an intelligence agent, and a decade later Aaron Burr apparently hoped to profit from surviving separatist sentiment in the West.

Spain was determined to hold as much of the east bank of the Mississippi as she could, to keep as much distance as possible between her territories and the ever more numerous American frontiersmen. Friendship with the Indians, particularly the Creeks, was carefully cultivated in the belief that they could aid in resisting American aggression. Because the United States under the Articles of Confederation had a weak, ineffective government and because Washington's government, after ratification of the Constitution in 1788, at first gave relatively low priority to opening the Mississippi, Spain's policy was successful for a decade. Paradoxically, during those same years, Americans were being encouraged to settle in areas claimed by Spain in the hope that they would help form a barrier against military attack from the United States.

The end of that policy came when Spain made peace with revolutionary France in Europe. Facing war with Great Britain, the Spanish government learned that the United States had negotiated an agreement (Jay's Treaty) with the British that settled some of the difficulties between the two English-speaking powers. Under those conditions it behooved the Spaniards to cultivate good relations with the United States so that Louisiana and Florida would not be threatened from land as well as by sea.

When Thomas Pinckney refused to enter an alliance with Spain for mutual protection of territories, a treaty satisfactory to the United States, known as Pinckney's Treaty or the Treaty of San Lorenzo, was negotiated. Spain accepted thirty-one degrees latitude as the southern boundary of the United States, thus fixing the northern boundary of that part of the state of Louisiana east of the Mississippi. The mutual right of Spanish and American citizens to navigate the entire length of the Mississippi was agreed upon, and United States citizens were given the right of deposit at New Orleans, though the place could be changed after three years. That was particularly important, because it meant that westerners shipping goods abroad could unload cargoes in New Orleans for transfer to ocean-going ships without paying Spanish duties. Attempted withdrawal of that right of deposit later contributed to the crisis leading to the Louisiana Purchase.

The importance of Louisiana to the United States during the Revolution should not be overestimated, but neither should it be discounted. Spanish aid had a definite effect on outcome of campaigns in the Northwest. Gálvez's campaigns not only brought Florida under Spanish control at war's end, but the troops that Britain used for the defense of Florida might otherwise have been thrown into the campaigns in the thirteen colonies. Postwar developments consolidated American control over the territory specified as belonging to the United States in the peace treaty. The settlement of that area by Anglo-Americans sealed the fate of Spanish Florida and of Spain's Indian allies, and the increase of Americans in the west, dependent upon the Mississippi for reaching their markets, made it inevitable that the United States should cast covetous eyes upon New Orleans in particular and Louisiana in general.

4

The Americanization of Louisiana

*L*OUISIANA was a French-speaking Spanish colony when the nineteenth century began. Twelve years later Louisiana was one of the United States, successfully operating a system of government radically different from the autocracy tempered by inefficiency that had gone before. The transition was quite rapid, and its accomplishment is one of the major achievements of American statecraft. It was also in large measure the accomplishment of a sometimes neglected American statesman, William C. C. Claiborne.

Available evidence does not show that the ideas of the American Revolution had any appreciable effect on the native people of Louisiana. On the other hand, the migration of Tories into the province did introduce into the population an element accustomed to a large degree of self-government. The ideas of the French Revolution had more effect, probably, because in the eighteenth century there was more cultural traffic between Louisiana and France than between Louisiana and the United States. The concept of "liberty, equality, and fraternity" appealed to a large enough minority that an enthusiastic crowd rioted in New Orleans streets when news arrived of the beheading of King Louis XVI.

French Santo Domingo, or Haiti, was a secondary source of revolutionary ideas. A slave revolt forced many whites and free blacks to flee from the island, and numbers of them came to

Louisiana, some bringing their slaves with them. Many of these refugees, especially the free blacks and slaves, had absorbed revolutionary ideas. Santo Domingan agitators were almost certainly responsible for a slave insurrection at Pointe Coupee in 1795. They were also blamed for a much more serious revolt in St. John the Baptist Parish sixteen years later. During the late 1790s, there was some talk of annexation to the United States, but the speakers were almost surely Anglo-Americans who had come down from the north.

In Europe, the late 1790s saw Napoleon Bonaparte become master of France. In the long run the people of Spain would do more than their share toward bringing Bonaparte down; but before 1800 the Spanish government had become a puppet manipulated by the French dictator. In the meantime, relations between France and the United States had deteriorated to such a point that in 1798 an undeclared naval war broke out. The friendship that had resulted from the American Revolution and from early American sympathy with the French Revolution was largely dissipated. The Federalists had long looked on revolutionary France with a jaundiced eye, and by the time of his election as president in 1800, Thomas Jefferson had come to see the nation whose culture he so much admired as a potentially dangerous enemy.

Jefferson's fears were not figments of his imagination. One of Bonaparte's ambitions was to restore France's empire in the New World, and Louisiana offered a beginning place for such a restoration. By the secret Treaty of San Ildefonso of 1800, Spain ceded Louisiana to France. It is often said that Napoleon forced the cession upon Spain, but it does not seem that a great deal of pressure was required. Louisiana had been as much of a white elephant in Spain's hands as it had been earlier in the hands of France. On the other hand, the Spanish government did get Bonaparte's promise that he would never transfer Louisiana to a third party.

The treaty was negotiated shortly before the Treaty of Amiens brought a short period of peace to Europe. The French dictator, well aware that war would soon break out again, hoped to use the peace to consolidate his new empire. Since England was almost sure to remain mistress of the seas, France must have a naval base in the Caribbean if she was to retain Louisiana. French Santo Domingo, or Haiti, was a natural site for such a naval base, but the slaves on the island, led by Toussaint L'Ouverture, had wrested control from their former masters.

Napoleon sent an army under his brother-in-law, General Charles Leclerc, to Haiti to put down the rebellion. Toussaint was treacherously captured when he went aboard a French ship under a flag of truce, but he had taught his followers well, and they waged ferocious guerrilla warfare against Leclerc's soldiers. Then a yellow fever epidemic reinforced the rebels; General Leclerc himself fell victim to the disease, and his army was soon reduced to impotence. There was no recourse but to transport the men who had survived back to France. Thus, France would be unable to hold Louisiana in case of renewed war with England.

Secret agreements between nations seldom remain secret for long, and Jefferson knew of the cession of Louisiana to France soon after he took office. He had no illusions about France's intentions; nor, in case of war between France and England, did he want New Orleans to fall into British hands. He wrote that whatever power held New Orleans was the "natural and habitual enemy" [1] of the United States. Leader of the radical faction that had led the thirteen colonies to revolution against Great Britain and to adoption of the Declaration of Independence, Jefferson also wrote: "The day that France takes possession of New Orleans . . . we must marry ourselves to the British fleet and nation." [2] General Leclerc's failure in Santo Domingo and the obvious imminence of renewed war in Europe made such a distasteful marriage unnecessary.

It is very doubtful that Bonaparte was the least bit frightened of the United States, but without control of Santo Domingo, he could not send to Louisiana the army he had planned to send. If

1. Thomas Jefferson to Robert Livingston, April 18, 1802, in *Basic Writings of Thomas Jefferson,* edited by Philip S. Foner (New York: Wiley Book Company, 1944), p. 656.
2. Jefferson to Livingston, April 18, 1802, in Foner, *Basic Writings,* p. 657.

the colony could not be defended, it would almost certainly be captured by the British when war broke out again. Thus he was receptive when the United States suggested that he sell New Orleans to the new republic.

Jefferson hoped to avoid war over the Mississippi if avoidance was at all possible. He instructed the American minister to France, Robert Livingston, to try to purchase the Isle of Orleans, and he obtained an appropriation of $2 million from Congress for that purpose. Also, he sent James Monroe to join Livingston in the negotiations. For months before Monroe's arrival, Livingston had been attempting to persuade the French to sell New Orleans. He had accomplished nothing because, as he informed Jefferson, the people with whom he dealt had no authority to make a decision. Only Bonaparte could do that.

However, when one man makes all decisions, policy can be changed very rapidly. In early April 1803, unwilling to see Louisiana taken by the British, Bonaparte decided to sell to the United States not only New Orleans, but the entire Louisiana colony. On April 8, Livingston was offered all the French holdings for one hundred million francs. Monroe arrived soon after, and after some haggling the two envoys made the purchase for sixty million francs, or about fifteen million dollars. It was probably the best real estate deal in all history. The United States had more than doubled its area, and it paid for the land, including the most important outlet to the Gulf of Mexico, only about four cents an acre.

The treaty of cession was vague as to boundaries, and Livingston suggested to Talleyrand, the French foreign minister, that it might be well to be more specific. Talleyrand admitted frankly that he did not know what the boundaries were but added: "You have made a noble bargain for yourselves and I suppose you will make the most of it." [3] Those were prophetic words.

President Jefferson was somewhat taken aback by the degree of success his envoys had achieved, but he soon recovered and

3. Robert Livingston to James Madison, May 20, 1803, quoted in E. Wilson Lyon, *Louisiana in French Diplomacy, 1759–1804* (Norman: University of Oklahoma Press, 1934), 225–226.

designated William C. C. Claiborne, then territorial governor of Mississippi, formerly congressman from Tennessee, to receive the new lands from France. General James Wilkinson, still on the Spanish payroll, was named to command the troops, mainly Mississippi militia, that accompanied Governor Claiborne. On November 30, Pierre Clément Laussat assumed control of the province for France, and in his few days of power abolished the Spanish government of New Orleans in favor of a mayor, Étienne de Boré, and a city council made up of Creoles and Americans. Claiborne, after a two-week march, reached a point three miles from the Place d'Armes, now Jackson Square, on December 17. Laussat set December 20 as the date for the ceremonial transfer.

On that day, the American troops marched into the city and formed opposite the French garrison in the Place d'Armes. Claiborne and Wilkinson were escorted into the Cabildo, where the formality of exchanging documents was carried out. Laussat absolved the people of the city from their loyalty to France and urged them to become American citizens. The final act of cession, written in English and French, was signed. Then the official party stood on the balcony of the Cabildo while, simultaneously, the French flag was lowered and the United States flag raised. Claiborne then made a short address, promising the people that they would be admitted to all the rights of American citizens as quickly as possible, and that they were immediately guaranteed "enjoyment of their liberty, property and religion." [4] Louisiana, a province extending from the Gulf to an undetermined Canadian boundary in the north and to a definitely nebulous meeting with Spanish territory to the west, had become part of the United States. Soon the Americans would claim that West Florida was part of Louisiana, thus proving Talleyrand a good, if perhaps cynical, prophet.

The people of Louisiana, except for the relatively few Americans there, were not overjoyed by the change of masters. Despite Claiborne's words, many devout Catholics feared that the

4. François Xavier Martin, *History of Louisiana* (1882; reprint ed., New Orleans: Pelican Publishing Co., 1963), p. 297.

Protestant United States would not allow them freedom of religion. In general, the people of New Orleans were not fond of Americans anyway. Last, but not least, soon after Claiborne took possession, Congress prohibited the importation of slaves into Louisiana from abroad, a measure that aroused the ire of the upper classes. Louisianians evaded that law whenever possible and bought large numbers of smuggled slaves, but their opinion of American government was not improved.

W. C. C. Claiborne was, for all practical purposes, dictator of Louisiana from December of 1803 until May of 1805. Theoretically, he was subordinate to the U.S. secretary of state and the president, and, eventually, to Congress; but in practice the time required for communication between Washington and New Orleans was so great that the governor had to use his own judgment in nearly all matters. Fortunately, Claiborne was a man of very good judgment, and he realized that his primary task was to conciliate the people over whom he ruled—a task at which he was remarkably successful.

Congress divided the Louisiana Purchase into the District of Louisiana north of the thirty-third parallel of latitude and the Territory of Orleans south of that line. Congress acted in March, but not until October was Claiborne inaugurated as governor of the unorganized Territory of Orleans. That did not lessen his power significantly; he was to have a legislative council appointed by President Jefferson to advise him, but the president sent Claiborne thirteen commissions, signed but otherwise blank, so the governor's council was hand-picked and co-operative.

The better-informed citizens of Louisiana knew that under the Northwest Ordinance of 1787 a territory with more than five thousand free white males was eligible to become an organized territory, and they resented their relegation to unorganized status. Étienne de Boré was so indignant that he resigned as mayor of New Orleans. Those who wanted a partly representative government did not have long to wait, however, because in 1805 Congress made Orleans into an organized territory. Claiborne remained governor by presidential appointment, and a five-man legislative council was also appointed, but from a list of ten names drawn up by an elected house of representatives of twenty-five members. For the first election of representatives, voters were required to have been citizens of the United States for three years and to own two hundred acres of land, but the first legislature reduced voter requirements to three months' citizenship and fifty acres of land. That was still a stringently restricted electorate, but it freely gave the vote to long-time inhabitants of Louisiana who owned property. Taking into consideration the fact that the people of Louisiana had had no experience in self-government, the gradual introduction of suffrage was probably wise. On the other hand, highly restricted suffrage persisted in Louisiana until 1845, longer than it should have.

The legislative council, attempting to give Louisiana a government like that of the southern states, in 1804 divided the territory into twelve counties, which served as electoral districts. Ecclesiastical parishes had been the vital unit of local administration under Spain, however, and the legislature created nineteen parishes. Gradually, the parishes became the units of local government; the counties continued to lead a somewhat shadowy existence until they were finally abolished in the Constitution of 1845. The same legislature that created the parishes provided that the parish judge, justices of the peace, and a jury of twelve citizens should meet together once a year to deal with roads, bridges, levees, and police matters, or keeping order within the parish. With the passage of time, the office of parish judge ceased to exist, the justices of the peace became purely judicial officers, and the jury, gradually becoming known as the police jury, became the administrative and legislative body of the parish. Obviously, government suited to rural parishes was not suited to the city of New Orleans. There, for the time being, Claiborne continued the government established by Laussat. Throughout Louisiana history, the government of the Crescent City has of necessity differed in form from other local units within the state.

In the beginning Claiborne kept in force all Spanish law that did not conflict with the United States Constitution, but common law was soon substituted for Spanish law in criminal cases;

and in 1808 a new civil law, based on the Napoleonic Code of France, was put into effect. Later, in 1825, a new adaptation of the Napoleonic Code was instituted, and it has remained as the basis of Louisiana's civil law to this day. A new slave code was largely a repetition of the French and Spanish *Code Noir,* though slightly more severe. The administration of justice was in the hands of justices of the peace, three so-called superior-court judges, and one United States district judge.

Claiborne was highly successful in conciliating the non-American people of the Territory of Orleans. He quickly convinced them that the United States would do nothing to interfere with their freedom of worship. Merchants and property owners, accustomed to Roman law, were pleased at its retention in civil matters. When the Mississippi militia that had come with him went home, Claiborne began creating a native militia as some protection against slave insurrections. He chose the original members of the militia carefully, but by forming it he demonstrated trust in the people, and his trust was reciprocated.

In 1805 former Vice-President Aaron Burr arrived in New Orleans and conferred with General Wilkinson and a number of leading citizens. Historians are still uncertain as to what Burr was planning. He said that he intended simply to settle a Spanish land grant. Andrew Jackson apparently believed that he planned a filibustering expedition against Spanish lands to the west. President Jefferson thought Burr planned to detach Louisiana and perhaps Tennessee and Kentucky from the Union and join them with Mexico into an empire that he would rule. Certainly General Wilkinson was implicated, though whether he participated in the hope of personal gain from the plot or in his role as a spy for Spain it is impossible to say. At any rate, in 1806, he denounced Burr to President Jefferson, declared martial law in New Orleans, and sent officers upriver to arrest Burr, who was descending the Mississippi with a party of armed men. Burr fled across country and was arrested in what is now Alabama. He was tried in Richmond and acquitted. It has been suggested that the Burr conspiracy, if it can be so called, was a last spark from the dying embers of the old Spanish Conspiracy of earlier years. Certainly Louisiana showed no overt interest in any move toward separation from the United States then or for years afterward.

The United States claimed that the western boundary of the Territory of Orleans was at least the Sabine River and suggested the Rio Grande; Spain insisted on a line just west of Natchitoches and extending southward to the Mermentau River. In 1804 war almost broke out between the two nations, but the fact that General Wilkinson was a Spanish spy may have served to preserve the peace. The opposing commanders agreed that neither nation would establish military posts in the disputed area east of the Sabine, thus creating a neutral strip thirty to forty miles wide. That strip became a haven for horse thieves and other outlaws who committed depredations in both American and Spanish territory. From time to time, either American or Spanish troops, each side always with the consent of the other, would sweep the strip to recover stolen property and fugitive slaves and occasionally to arrest men wanted for crimes by one nation or the other. The western boundary was finally fixed at the Sabine River by the Adams-Onís Treaty of 1819.

To the east, the United States had claimed the area between the Mississippi and Perdido rivers (West Florida) from the time of the Louisiana Purchase, but no military action was taken. Jefferson and his successor, James Madison, could afford to be patient. Many Americans had migrated into the area south of the thirty-first parallel; indeed, few people other than emigrants from the United States lived in that part of West Florida near and north of Baton Rouge. These people were not in any way oppressed by the Spanish, but they did want to live under the American flag. In the fall of 1810, some seventy armed men, led by Philemon Thomas, rode south from St. Francisville and, after a sharp but short battle, forced the surrender of Baton Rouge on September 23. As soon as he learned of the revolt, President James Madison ordered Claiborne to take possession of West Florida. Claiborne moved rapidly and organized four parishes between the Mississippi and Pearl rivers, in an area thereafter described as the Florida Parishes. Mobile remained in Spanish hands until it was occupied by General Wilkinson at the beginning of the War of 1812, but the strip of Florida between the Pearl and Perdido rivers was attached to Mississippi and Alabama territories and never became part of Louisiana. Talleyrand's prophetic abilities were further confirmed.

The census of 1810 showed that the Territory of Orleans, not including West Florida, had a population of more than 76,000 people, and in early 1811, Congress authorized a constitutional convention. The convention met in a New Orleans coffeehouse affording ample room for the thirty-seven delegates. Julien Poydras was elected chairman of the convention, which, if one can judge by the names, had more than twice as many delegates of French ancestry as there were Anglo-Americans. Even so, the convention adopted a constitution that was the same as that of Kentucky, with only slight variations. The new constitution limited suffrage to adult males who owned property and/or paid taxes, provided a two-year term for a twenty-five-man house of representatives, and called for a senate of fourteen men elected to four-year terms. The governor served a four-year term, but could not succeed himself. An interesting feature of the constitution was that the people voted for candidates for governor, but that the final choice was to be made by the legislature between the two candidates with the highest number of votes. It should be added here that the legislature under the Constitution of 1812 always elected the candidate with the highest number of popular votes. The governor was far stronger than most governors in the Union, having the power, with senate approval, to appoint all judges and local officials.

The constitution as drawn up did not include the Florida Parishes within the boundaries of the proposed new state of Louisiana, but the convention adopted a resolution requesting that that territory be added to the new state. Congress complied with the request, and on April 30, 1812, Louisiana, including the Florida Parishes, became the eighteenth state of the Union. In the first election, Claiborne received almost three thousand votes and Jacques Villeré less than one thousand. The legislature then selected Claiborne, so that this remarkable man governed Louisiana for thirteen years, longer than any of his successors up to 1976.

Nine years of Caliborne's administration had done much to

accustom the people of Louisiana to representative government. Some of the more prominent natives were rapidly learning the game of American politics. For as long as possible, they clung to their Gallic culture, but they adapted quickly to the new political system. The attachment of the people of Louisiana to the United States would be sharply reinforced later, in the smoke of battle, for Louisiana had joined a Union that was about to go to war.

This is not the place for a history of the War of 1812. The early campaigns took place along the Canadian border, and their only real importance to Louisiana was that General Wilkinson, given a command in that area, proved utterly incompetent and disappeared from history. He was replaced in the Southwest by Andrew Jackson of Tennessee, whose lack of formal military training was compensated for by instinct, intelligence, and an iron will. Jackson would later direct a campaign in which the people of Louisiana and the United States would be fused together finally and inextricably.

After Bonaparte's first surrender in Europe, a British army made up in large part of veterans of the Peninsular Campaign and commanded by the Duke of Wellington's brother-in-law, Sir Edward Pakenham, was assembled in Jamaica and ordered to take New Orleans. Jackson was sure that a British landing on the Gulf Coast was coming, but it was not until late November of 1814 that he decided that New Orleans was the objective. In Europe a treaty of peace had been under negotiation since August of 1814, but neither Jackson nor Pakenham knew about it. Furthermore, the treaty was not signed until December 24, 1814, and was not ratified in the United States until February 17, 1815; had the results of the New Orleans campaign been different, it might never have been ratified. Thus, at least from the American point of view, the Battle of New Orleans was not the useless struggle it has sometimes been called.

Jackson set about obstructing approaches to the Crescent City as best he could. Defense of the Mississippi River approach was obviously necessary and was attended to. The mouth of Bayou Lafourche, which could have brought the British into the Mississippi above New Orleans, was blocked. The Rigolets, which provided an approach to Lake Pontchartrain from Lake Borgne, were obstructed. Troops were stationed to oppose any landing from Lake Pontchartrain, should the British nonetheless manage to bring their fleet into that body of water. The British had much better maps than Jackson had, and they had planned from the beginning to move from Lake Borgne up Bayou Bienvenue, which would bring them to the high ground next to the Mississippi at Chalmette, a few miles south of New Orleans. Only a small company of militia, including Major Gabriel Villeré, was stationed at Chalmette, and it was captured. Major Villeré escaped by leaping through a window and taking to his heels. Making his way to New Orleans, he told Jackson that a large part of the British army had already taken up positions south of the city.

Jackson had arrived at New Orleans with a few hundred regular troops and about as many militia, but this strength grew rapidly. The Louisiana militia was called up, and their willingness to fight for the United States demonstrated that Claiborne had done his work of reconciliation well. In the militia were two battalions of free black men, and slaves did much of the work in constructing Jackson's fortifications. Important in song and story, and also to history, is the fact that Jackson finally accepted the proffered assistance of Jean Laffite (more commonly spelled *Lafitte*) and his privateers from the islands at the entrance to Barataria Bay. They played an important part in the Battle of New Orleans, providing crews for two naval craft in the river and manning some of Jackson's artillery. On the eve of battle, more than two thousand Tennessee and Kentucky riflemen joined Jackson. He even had somewhat more than a hundred Choctaw warriors.

As soon as he learned of the British approach, Jackson chose a spot for his defensive line where the river and the swamp were but fifteen hundred yards apart. His problem was to prevent an enemy attack while he prepared his fortifications. His solution was to order something rare in American military annals: a night attack on the enemy camp. The attackers used rifle butts, knives, and tomahawks more than powder and shot; their yells convinced many of the British that they were set upon by Indians. Casualties were evenly divided—about two hundred killed, wounded, or missing for each army—but the attack served Jackson's purpose. The British concluded that they had better wait until their full force had arrived, since the Americans were so eager to give battle, and the pause gave Jackson the time he needed.

Because only relatively small boats could navigate Bayou Bienvenue, the British were limited in the amount of artillery and artillery ammunition they could bring to the battlefield. On December 28, Pakenham tested the American lines and was driven back with heavy casualties. Then, on January 1, 1815, he sought to batter a hole in Jackson's earthworks with artillery fire—a move somewhat embarrassing to Jackson, because, when the bombardment began, his men were out of the lines on dress parade, but the challenge was quickly accepted. No impression was made on the fortifications, and apparently all of Jackson's guns survived to play their role in the climactic battle of January 8.

Hindsight makes it clear now that the failure of the New Year's Day bombardment meant the failure of the British campaign against New Orleans, but General Pakenham did not have the benefit of more than a century and a half of hindsight. He had an army of five to six thousand men who had demonstrated their discipline and courage time and again in campaigns against the French in Portugal and Spain. He outnumbered Jackson by five to three, and most of Jackson's men were militia who had had little or no experience in battle. Finally, Pakenham could hardly have come so far, put his army in position, and then gone home without fighting a major battle. Nor could he stay where he was; idleness and disease would soon ruin his fine army. Therefore, he ordered a full-scale attack on the American position for the morning of January 8, 1815.

Errors were made by the British, particularly the fact that ladders were not brought forward for mounting the American earthworks, but it is most unlikely that the results would have been different had there been no errors. No praise of the courage of the British officers and men could be too great. As soon as an early-morning fog cleared, they advanced in perfect formation, suffering heavy casualties from American artillery fire. The closer they came to the American lines, the more deadly was the fire from Jackson's cannon; then, at close range, the riflemen were permitted to fire at will. Not all frontiersmen could hit a squirrel at fifty yards, but many of them could; the crossed belts of the British uniforms provided an almost perfect aiming point. Indeed, it was more of a slaughter than a battle; the British lost more than two thousand men, including a disproportionate number of officers, one of whom was General Pakenham himself. Jackson's casualties had been almost unbelievably light— seventy-one men—of whom only six or seven were killed.

The British remained in position for another ten days, mainly to bury their dead and care for men too badly wounded to move. On January 18 they left their camp and by January 27 were back aboard ship. However, the fleet remained in the Gulf, and Jackson kept in effect the martial law he had declared on December 16, believing that the British attack might be renewed from another quarter. Because of that he was severely criticized by many, but especially by one Louis Louaillier. Jackson had Louaillier placed under military arrest, but Federal District Judge Dominick Hall ordered his release. Jackson's response was to place Judge Hall and District Attorney John Dick under arrest. On March 13 Jackson learned of the peace treaty and declared martial law at an end. Upon being released, Dick promptly brought suit against Jackson in Judge Hall's court, and Hall fined Jackson one thousand dollars. Jackson paid the fine; but many years later Congress restored the money, with interest.

The Battle of New Orleans marked the completion of the political Americanization of Louisiana. Instead of fear and resentment of the United States, Louisianians had come to think of themselves as citizens of the young republic. Instead of regarding voting and jury duty as impositions, they had come to exercise the one zestfully and accept the other, albeit with some reluctance. Hostility between French and Anglo persisted, but it was rivalry within a system accepted by both. For political and economic reasons, more and more French-speaking people of the state were learning English. The Creole and the Acadian would hold strongly to their culture, especially their religion, their diet, and their recreation; the last two came to be adopted by more and more American settlers; and as a result of marriage vows, more and more sons and daughters of Americans became Catholics. Politically, however, by 1815 Louisiana was one of the southern United States. It was different, even unique, but it was part of the Union, not an occupied province. Claiborne, who died in 1817, soon after being elected to the United States Senate, had done his work well.

5

Moonlight, Magnolias, Moneymaking, and Politics in Antebellum Louisiana

$\mathcal{T}$HE population of Louisiana grew from perhaps fifty thousand to more than seven hundred thousand in the years between the Louisiana Purchase and the outbreak of the Civil War. By 1860, a class system had become more or less firmly fixed, headed by a merchant-planter oligarchy and based upon a mudsill of black slaves. New Orleans was the greatest port and the largest city in the South; and in the country, plantations came to dominate agriculture. The slave system became more rigorous as plantation agriculture developed and as Louisianians became more aware of abolitionist agitation against slavery. Politics began basically as a contest between Anglo-American and French, then developed into a version of national party politics modified by Louisiana circumstances. As the antebellum period drew to an end, the slavery question dissolved the Whig Party and came more and more to dominate politics until the political climate was ready for the secession crisis.

Like the rest of the antebellum South, Louisiana is sometimes imagined, a century later, as suffused in a soft golden glow made up of equal parts of nostalgia and moonlight. Tall, handsome gentlemen bow to beautiful ladies in crinoline; the sweet odor of magnolia blossoms fills the air; and the sound of a banjo is heard, far enough removed in time and space to make soft music for the singing of contented slaves. Such an image is even more seductive in the case of Louisiana, because the handsome gentlemen may be speaking French, and the ladies, answering in the same romantic tongue, are small, dark, and vivacious, possessed of all the virtues of their Anglo-Saxon sisters elsewhere in the South, but with the spicy tang of Latinism added. Away from the Big House and the slave quarter stretch endless cotton and cane fields, surrounded by trees bowed down with Spanish moss, with here and there a cabin from which comes the sound of a fiddle playing an Acadian tune, sung by a large, happy illiterate family in an appealing patois.

There is some element of reality in this dream. From the Arkansas border down the west bank of the Mississippi was rich, black, alluvial soil extending inward to merge with similar soil deposited by tributaries of the Red River. The soil in the narrow valley of the Red was not black, but it was equally fertile, and it extended to and beyond the Louisiana-Texas border. Such lands were ideal for cotton planting. Equally good soil was found on both sides of the Mississippi below the mouth of the Red River and along the bayous to the west, especially Bayou Lafourche and Bayou Teche. In the northern part of that area, either sugar or cotton might be cultivated, but most of South Louisiana was sugar country, and great sugar plantations were as common on the good soils as were cotton plantations to the north.

In all the state in 1860, there were about 1,600 plantations with more than fifty slaves each. One parish, Tensas on the upper Mississippi, had 118 such plantations. These agricultural units with fifty or more slaves encompassed more than 43 percent of the state's arable land. The number of plantations employing twenty or more slaves—a count frequently and arbitrarily used to distinguish plantation from farm—was obviously much greater. The count does not, however, make Louisiana into a land of feudal lords and ladies. Half the people were black, and the vast majority of these black people were slaves without hope of anything better for themselves or their children.

Even free blacks were an inferior caste, legally, subject to restrictions that were, to say the least, demeaning.

Of the state's white people, the vast majority belonged either to the middle class or the working class. New Orleans supported a large urban middle class made up of lawyers, clerks, physicians, shopkeepers, skilled artisans, and practitioners of many other occupations. These people varied in the degree of prosperity attained, but as a whole, they were literate, conservative, religious, and economically ambitious. A prominent historian has noted that "Wealth was the all-consuming aim of practically everyone in the community." [1] These middle-class people might be of almost any Caucasian origin, but Protestant Anglo-Americans and foreign-born French from either the West Indies or France seem to have outstripped the *ancienne population*—that is, those citizens of New Orleans descended from settlers who had arrived during the colonial period. In more sparsely settled areas, merchants, lawyers, parish officials, and better-off artisans made up a small-town middle class that complemented the urban middle class of New Orleans.

Finally, it must not be thought that the countryside was inhabited only by great planters and their slaves on the one hand and half-starved poor whites on the other. The great planters did dominate the countryside—for that matter, they dominated the state as a whole; but the less important planters and the more prosperous yeoman farmers definitely made up a rural middle class. Most Louisiana farmers were yeoman who engaged primarily in subsistence agriculture. They planted some cotton, and occasionally, in the southern part of the state, some sugar as a source of cash, but basically they concentrated on growing the corn and livestock upon which their familes subsisted. In North Louisiana the yeoman was almost always Anglo-American; in the southern part of the state, he was more likely to be Acadian or a descendant of earlier settlers of the colonial period.

In North Louisiana, small farms were mainly located in the hills lying north of the Red River; in the western part of the

1. Joseph G. Tregle, "Early New Orleans Society: A Reappraisal," *Journal of Southern History* 18 (February 1952):28.

state, they lay south of the Red. There were, however, many yeoman farmers interspersed among the planters in the more fertile lowlands, and they dominated agriculture in the eastern parts of the Florida Parishes. In the south, it was common for planter and small farmer to live side by side. Because of the large investment required for sugar production, small cultivators did not usually attempt that crop.

Drawing a line between the poorer yeoman farmer and the poor white in the countryside was difficult. Probably it was as much a matter of social standing and attitude as of economic status. The poor white was more likely to live in pine hills, but he might be found in rich plantation country. Not much is known about economic distinctions among rural Acadians, but there were Acadians, and other Latins, who were economically and culturally more deprived than was normal; their way of life, like that of the Anglo-American poor white farther north, could almost be called degraded. It should be emphasized that such people made up a relatively small proportion of the white population. The poor of New Orleans had been present from the founding of the city, but they grew in numbers during the 1840s and 1850s with the arrival of large numbers of Irish and German immigrants. These immigrants were not only important as a source of manual labor in the city; they were also important politically, often holding the balance of power between the generally opposed French and American factions.

At the bottom of New Orleans society were Negroes. The Crescent City had a large community of free Negroes, some of them wealthy and cultured, able to send their children to private schools, give liberally to the Catholic church, and contribute significantly to the well-being of the city. The philanthropies of Thomy Lafon led to the raising of a statue to commemorate his good works. Other free blacks, however, made up a sort of underworld, living by their wits and frequently behaving in a manner that was, to say the least, unruly.

The slaves of New Orleans were perhaps the most sophisticated group of bondsmen since the days of ancient Rome. Most of them were either domestic servants or workers in some skilled occupation; waiters, draymen, bricklayers, carpenters, and blacksmiths could be slaves. Many managed their own affairs, paying their masters an agreed-upon share of their earnings; in the early part of the antebellum period, many such blacks were able to save enough to buy first their own freedom and then that of their spouses and children. Those who remained slaves with no hope of emancipation were not docile automatons, but rather men and women who knew something of the world, and who knew that in large numbers they could assert a degree of independence that was impossible for one of them acting alone.

In evaluating antebellum Louisiana society, it must be remembered that most of the state was still frontier or barely past the frontier stage in 1860. The hills of North Louisiana were very thinly settled until after the Civil War, and the plantations of much of the state were on land that had been wilderness only a short time before. Few of these plantations had columned mansions; most of the elaborate homes that attract tourists today were completed in the last ten years before the Civil War. Louisiana planter society, with few exceptions, was not an aristocracy; rather, it was a society of self-made men. Late in the period, the acquistion of increased wealth and, perhaps, the leisure for reading Sir Walter Scott's novels had brought some posturing of gentility to the countryside; but basically, successful planters were businessmen whose business was producing cotton or sugar with slave labor.

It must be emphasized that although antebellum Louisiana most definitely had a class system, the lines between social and economic classes were not unscalable among whites. Many instances could be cited of yeoman farmers who through luck, ability, and hard work became great planters, or of clerks who worked their way upward to become successful, well-to-do factors. Many other instances could be cited of once-wealthy men who lost all that they had. It was characteristic of the South, however, that the bankrupt family of social status retained that status for a time even after the wealth on which it had originally been based had disappeared.

The location of New Orleans near the mouth of the Mississippi put that city in a position to exact commercial tribute from almost the entire region between the Appalachians and the Rocky Mountains, so long as water was the most practical means of transporting goods in bulk. The city was perhaps the most unhealthful in the nation. Its streets were lower than the normal level of the Mississippi and could be flooded by a break in the levee or a heavy rain. Hurricanes struck from time to time, sometimes flooding the streets with salt water from Lake Pontchartrain. Epidemics, all too frequent, were deadly. There were no sewers except the ditches beside the usually unpaved streets. Despite all that, the city hummed with business. The greatest amount of trade was carried on in the fall and winter, when the harvest was coming in from upriver; but during the spring orders for goods from planters in the city's hinterland kept merchants busy. Bankers, importers, exporters, and merchants all played an essential part in the city's economy, and factors played the most important role of all.

While the planter remained on his plantation concentrating on the production of sugar or cotton, the factor served as his business agent in New Orleans. The planter shipped his crop to the factor after the harvest; the factor worked to get the best possible price for it, in return for which he received a commission, usually 2½ percent. The remainder of the amount received was credited to the planter's account with the factor, from whom the planter ordered such supplies as he needed until the next crop came in. If the planter needed cash, he wrote a draft upon his factor. The factor also charged a commission on purchases he made for his customers, and if, as was often the case, the planter ran up a bigger bill than his crop would cover, the factor collected interest on the unpaid balance. In the nature of things, many factors who were successful became plantation owners; indeed, many of them had family ties with the planters they served.

The services of New Orleans to its hinterland were not all economic. Any form of recreation, legal or illegal, moral or immoral, was normally available there, before the Civil War as well as after. Gambling houses and saloons abounded, and bawdy houses catered to every level of taste and pocketbook. Already the city was famous for its cuisine, and all frequent visitors had a favorite restaurant. The St. Charles Hotel was nationally known for its luxury. The upper classes engaged in a most active social life, including dinners, balls, and other entertainments that reached a climax each year in the Mardi Gras celebration preceding the Lenten season. Many sugar and cotton planters were to a greater or lesser extent a part of New Orleans society, so that the city's cultural and social influence radiated out, as did its economic influence.

The planters closest to New Orleans grew sugar. Sugar cane was an exotic crop for Louisiana. The natural growing season for the plant was well over twelve months, but the Louisiana climate permitted only about nine months' growth. Thus it was necessary to develop a process for making sugar from immature cane, which had a much lower sugar content than the mature cane of the West Indies. Early attempts at solving the problem failed, but in the late eighteenth century Étienne de Boré successfully crystallized sugar from cane grown on his plantation.

Normally the sugar harvest was completed not later than mid-January. The canes themselves were the "seed" for sugar cane, and some of the seed cane might be cut before the regular harvest began. Some of it might even be planted before the harvest began, but that was not common in antebellum years. After a holiday following the harvest, plantation slaves were put to work preparing the soil for the next year's crop. Rows were thrown up about six feet apart, and the stalks of seed cane were laid flat in a shallow furrow made by running a light plow down the top of the row. New plants came up from each joint of the seed cane. Corn to serve as food for man and beast was also planted, and once the plowing was over, the plantation slaves spent the remainder of the spring and early summer hoeing the crop, destroying grass and weeds that might compete with the cane or corn for nourishment. By the Fourth of July, traditionally, though in practice it might be weeks earlier or later, the corn and cane had grown tall and strong enough to fend for themselves, and the crop was "laid by."

On a sugar plantation, laying by the crop did not mean a vacation, although the slaves were often given a day off at this time. The early summer was used for cutting wood from the swamp that lay behind every sugar plantation, to provide fuel for making sugar. When the wood-gathering was done, ditches were cleaned, levees repaired or strengthened, and—early in the century—perhaps some new ground was cleared for cultivation. In the enervating humidity of mid-summer in South Louisiana, clearing new ground was hard work and dangerous to health. As slave prices rose and immigration during the 1840s brought in large numbers of Irish immigrants, many planters preferred to hire immigrants for such work, usually at a dollar a day. If an Irishman sickened and died, there was one less Paddy in a world that seemed to have too many. If a slave died, the planter had lost perhaps more than a thousand dollars in invested capital and a laborer who had already learned the skills needed in making a sugar crop.

The cane harvest and sugar making, still referred to in Louisiana as "the grinding," was an industrial process as much as it was agricultural. Once the harvest began, work continued on a twenty-four-hour basis, though cutting cane in the fields was restricted to daylight hours. On some plantations eight-hour shifts, or "watches," were organized. Adult slaves worked two such shifts. In the fields, slaves cut the cane with special cane knives—something like a machete with a hook on the end—an operation requiring a high degree of skill. The worker had to cut the cane blades away from the stalk, lop off the top of the stalk, then sever it from the roots at ground level. Skilled hands did the job with little wasted motion. This writer has watched present-day cane-cutters at work, after a storm had tangled cane stalks so that machinery could not be efficiently used, and the motions of the work are almost as intricate as a ballet, and as rhythmical.

Other workers loaded the stalks upon two-wheeled carts for movement to the sugar house. Rainy weather could make that backbreaking work for men and animals as the heavily loaded carts cut the farm roads into a veritable morass. Fortunately, fall weather in Louisiana is usually good, October and November being the most pleasant months of the year. At the mill the cane was unloaded from the carts and fed into the press, two heavy, steam-powered iron cylinders that rolled against one another and squeezed the juice from the stalks. What was left of the cane, called *bagasse,* was sometimes dried and used as fuel for the mill, but more often it was, for all practical purposes, waste. The actual process of making sugar was too intricate to be described here in detail. It consisted, in essence, of boiling off more and more water from the juice, leaving a higher and higher sugar content in the remaining syrup, and then crystallizing the sugar. The molasses drained as residue was a salable by-product. Sugar produced on the plantation was brown sugar; it was loaded into hogsheads—large barrels holding a thousand pounds—and was shipped to the planter's factor in New Orleans for sale.

The plantation represented a sizable investment. Sugar lands were worth up to a hundred dollars per acre, the swamp in back ten dollars per acre; and the slaves needed to make the crop represented an expense at least equal to the cost of the land. The sugar mill was an additional major item of expense, to which had to be added the cost of work animals, agricultural tools, slave housing, and miscellaneous items. It was not at all unusual for the total investment in an antebellum sugar plantation to exceed $200,000. Even so, it was profitable. A careful analysis indicates that the return from sugar plantations in the 1850s was about 9 percent.

Cotton was suited to much more of Louisiana than was sugar. The pine hills and pine flats were too infertile for farming, and before the Civil War the prairies of Southwest Louisiana were used almost entirely for cattle grazing, but cotton was grown over almost all the remainder of North Louisiana and the Florida Parishes. Before 1820 cotton was planted frequently in what became the sugar parishes, but sugar proved more profitable that far south. Cotton was a crop that could be successfully grown by a planter with broad acres or by a slaveless yeoman farmer whose small patch provided a little cash for necessities and perhaps a few modest luxuries that could not be produced on his farm. Cotton planting did not require so large an investment as did sugar planting, and there was no shortage of land. Therefore, since labor was relatively expensive and land was cheap, the cotton planter attempted to produce as much cotton as possible per worker rather than per acre. That practice led to rapid exhaustion of the soil except along rivers and bayous, where frequent flooding deposited silt that maintained fertility; but at the time, that did not matter. More land could always be cleared and brought under the plow. Indeed, many cotton planters in Louisiana, or their fathers, had already exhausted lands farther east.

The fields of a cotton plantation were plowed as soon as weather permitted in late winter or early spring. Usually the corn crop was planted before the cotton. Because cold or wet weather might reduce germination, the cotton farmer sowed far more seed than the number of plants he would need, and in an ordinary year the first operation after planting consisted of thinning the cotton, at the same time hoeing out any grass or weeds growing with the cotton plants. The cotton might have to be hoed—an operation usually referred to as "chopping cotton"—several more times, depending upon how much rain fell.

Late in June or early in July, when cotton had grown tall and thick enough to shade out grass and therefore to survive without additional cultivation, it was laid by. As on sugar plantations, the Fourth of July was the traditional "lay-by" date. Normally, bolls containing cotton lint and seed then appeared on cotton plants. The bolls grew during the long summer days until they reached the size of a golf ball. As summer drew to an end, the plants began to die, and less and less moisture reached the bolls. As the lint inside dried, it pushed ever harder against the restraining walls of the boll. One day—in August, ordinarily—the bolls began to open, and in a few weeks, the fields were white with cotton.

At that time the field hands, who had been harvesting corn and gathering firewood for winter, began the hardest work of the year, picking cotton. It was a task that could be done by almost everyone, from small children to feeble old men and women, although naturally the strong and healthy could pick more than the weak. But strength and endurance were not the only important qualities in cotton-picking. Other characteristics, especially manual dexterity, played important roles. It has been said many times that the average picker could pick two hundred pounds of cotton a day, but Louisiana plantation records show that one hundred and fifty pounds would be closer to the average amount picked per day by the average adult slave. On the other hand, there were pickers, some of them women, who could pick three hundred, four hundred, and perhaps even five hundred pounds on a good day in a good field.

When about fourteen hundred pounds of cotton had been accumulated, it was ready for ginning—ready, that is, for the lint to be separated from the seed. The development of the cotton gin by Eli Whitney in 1793 had made large-scale cotton production feasible. Once the seed had been removed, the lint cotton was pressed into bales. After the Civil War, the standard bale grew to five hundred pounds, but in antebellum days, four hundred pounds was the normal weight. Once baled, cotton was ready for market, but getting it there was another matter. If the plantation was on the Mississippi River or the lower Red River, all that was necessary was to move the cotton to the landing and wait a few hours, or at most a few days, until a steamboat came by on the way to New Orleans. If the farm or plantation was far up the Red or on one of the smaller rivers or bayous, steamboats could not approach until a time of high water, so the producer might have to wait months before he could dispose of his crop.

Cotton planting in Louisiana, like sugar planting, was profitable. The total investment for fifteen hundred acres of land, four hundred of it in cultivation, with necessary slaves, animals, and equipment, was sometimes less than $100,000. Cotton prices varied with time and with the quality of the product, but the price was more often above than below eight cents per pound. At this price a fifteen-hundred-acre plantation would normally return a profit of about 7 percent on investment. Planters could go bankrupt, and they did, but not because cotton planting was inherently unprofitable. Some men were poor managers; some were operating on money borrowed at high interest rates and did not earn enough to meet the interest charges; some made good profits but persisted in spending more than they earned. Overall, however, growing sugar and cotton in Louisiana was profitable enough that the common ambition to become a planter was not at all misplaced.

Corn was the basic food for man and beast in Louisiana agriculture, and the growing of corn was essential to the production
of cotton and sugar. Occasionally planters concentrated on sugar
or cotton production and bought corn and pork from upriver, but
such men were relatively few in number, and the practice was
seldom long continued. Corn could be grown more efficiently in
the Middle West, but the making of a corn crop did not ordinarily take away labor needed in the sugar or cotton fields. The
same slaves could grow corn as well as the staple crop in which
the plantation specialized.

Cattle and swine were grown for food, and milch cows—
usually of rather low quality—were kept on plantations and
small farms. It was practically impossible to improve the quality
of cattle or swine, because for at least part of the year they were
allowed to run free in the forests and swamps, and many were
rounded up only to be branded, killed, or driven to market. The
free-ranging hogs were almost, if not quite, feral, and a special
breed of dog, the Catahoula hog-dog, was developed for catch-
ing them. True open-range cattle-grazing existed on the grassy
prairies of Southwest Louisiana, dating from Spanish colonial
days, and cattle continued to be the chief product of that area
until the introduction of rice-growing after the Civil War.

Early in the nineteenth century, oxen were almost the only
draft animals used for the heavy work in Louisiana agriculture.
Most people rode native "Creole" horses, lightweight animals
that also pulled buggies and light wagons. Horses bred from
eastern stock served as mounts for planters and pulled carriages
and fancy rigs. In the first part of the century, plows, farm
wagons and carts, and other heavy burdens were pulled by the
immensely strong but aggravatingly slow oxen. As the years
wore on, however, mules became more and more the preferred
draft animals on plantations, though oxen continued to play an
important role in Louisiana agriculture long after the Civil War.
Mules were much more expensive than oxen, and they were not
so strong, but they moved much faster. Also, they were pre-
sumed to be more intelligent, although any farmer knew that the
mule's intelligence was not always exercised in the interest of
his owner.

It is difficult today to comprehend how completely the life of the people of antebellum Louisiana was ordered by the cycle of crop production. The season of the year determined what clothes people wore, what food they ate, what work they did, what recreation they had. Certainly the activities of the man on the soil—planter, farmer, or slave—were determined largely by the growing of cotton, corn, or sugar, and that was also true of the dwellers in the state's little towns and smaller hamlets, whose primary function was to serve the farms and plantations surrounding them. Even in New Orleans, business activity was keyed to agricultural activity over the great valley of the Mississippi, which was as it should be, because New Orleans existed to serve agriculture just as much as did the smallest village. Fishermen and hunters who lived in the swamps and marshes along the Gulf of Mexico were independent of cotton and sugar, perhaps, but they were quite as subject to the rhythm of the seasons as any farmer.

Antebellum roads in Louisiana were so poor as hardly to deserve the name, and that situation did not improve markedly until the twentieth century. In the beginning, travelers followed blazed trails through the woods; but in time, increasing traffic marked the most favored routes on the earth's surface. Such roads were passable, however, only in good weather; and in summer, even in good weather, they were so dusty that riding them could be almost suffocating. The best roads in South Louisiana were along the banks of the Mississippi or one of the bayous where the ground was highest, but even those routes became quagmires in wet weather. Roads in the swamps were more often wet than dry, and for months at a time they might be under water. In North Louisiana the density of population was much less, and there were not so many roads, but such as there were were little, if any, better than those to the south. Only valuable goods of little bulk could be economically moved by road, and Louisiana produced little that answered that description.

Water transportation was without question the most important means of moving goods from one place to another. Louisiana was blessed with thousands of miles of navigable streams, and even small bayous that were not navigable for most of the year became so during times of high water. Plantations and commercial farms were almost of necessity located on watercourses, because otherwise there was no way of getting their produce to market. The most important streams, of course, were the Mississippi, the Red and its tributaries, the Black and Ouachita rivers, and, in the south, Bayous Lafourche, Terrebonne, and Teche. The Atchafalaya, from its origin at the junction of the Mississippi and the Red to the Gulf of Mexico, ran through almost impenetrable swamp and had no plantations along its course.

Rafts, flatboats, and keelboats were used on the Mississippi River almost from the time the first Anglo-American settlers crossed the Appalachians, and such craft continued to bring some produce to New Orleans throughout the antebellum years. Steamboat traffic began in 1812, when the *New Orleans,* built in Pittsburgh, came down the river. The *New Orleans* was really a keelboat powered by a single-cylinder, low-pressure steam engine, and the engine was not powerful enough to drive it back upstream to the Ohio. In 1814 Captain Henry Miller Shreve brought a similar but more powerful craft, the *Enterprise,* down from Pittsburgh, and the *Enterprise* huffed and puffed its way back to Louisville in twenty-five days.

These craft, though they were the first steamboats on the Mississippi, were not the prototypes of the steamers soon to become the chief means of river transportation. In 1816 Captain Shreve had the *Washington* built. Its hull was modeled upon the flatboat, and a high-pressure steam engine was mounted upon the lower of two decks, rather than in the hold. In 1817 the *Washington* made the round trip from New Orleans to Louisville in the remarkable time of forty-one days. The *Washington* and its thousands of descendants could carry a heavy cargo, yet their draft was so shallow that it was said that they could sail upon a heavy dew. Some were floating palaces, affording almost any luxury desired by first-class passengers, but it was as carriers of grain, cotton, sugar, and other goods to New Orleans that they made their great contribution to the economy of Louisiana.

In addition to developing the river steamer, Captain Shreve

made other contributions to navigation. He designed and put into use the first snag boat, a vessel that removed from the Mississippi snags capable of ripping the bottom out of a steamboat. Also, in the 1830s, he removed enough of the "Red River raft," a huge log jam blocking navigation for more than a hundred miles above Natchitoches, to permit river traffic to flow almost to the Texas border. During the last stages of that operation, Captain Shreve made his camp on Bennett's Bluff, and the town that grew up there was named Shreveport in his honor.

The first railroads were built in Louisiana shortly before the Panic of 1837. The early lines were short; the Pontchartrain went from the Mississippi River in New Orleans to Lake Pontchartrain, and the Mexican Gulf line ran from New Orleans to Lake Borgne. Farther north the West Feliciana connected St. Francisville with nearby Woodville, Mississippi, and the Clinton and Port Hudson joined those two places. Roads built in the 1850s were much more significant. The New Orleans, Jackson, and Great Northern stretched northward to Canton, Mississippi, before the Civil War and provided connections with Memphis and most major cities east of the Mississippi River. The New Orleans, Opelousas, and Great Western was greater in name than in fact; its tracks stopped at Brashear City, now Morgan City, and never attained Opelousas. The Vicksburg, Shreveport, and Texas was also more ambitious in name than in achievement. Beginning on the Mississippi opposite Vicksburg, it ended at Monroe on the Ouachita. The Baton Rouge, Grosse Tete, and Opelousas reached Livonia, perhaps twenty-five miles west of Baton Rouge by the route it followed. Not until after 1880 was the rail network of Louisiana improved significantly over what had existed in 1860.

In the final analysis, the economy of antebellum Louisiana was based upon slavery, and any discussion of the history of the state must give attention to the "peculiar institution." Although slavery in the United States ended only a little more than a century ago, it is difficult for most modern Americans to comprehend what it really was. It was a system under which human beings were things to be bought or sold, as cows or horses were bought and sold. Although he was theoretically protected by law against cruelty, the slave actually had only such protection as public opinion and his master's need for his labor gave him. One who sets out to find them can discover myriads of instances of inhuman cruelty to slaves, but the relative rarity of such instances says much for the comparative decency of most human beings and for the pervasiveness of the profit motive.

The main effort to relieve Louisiana's labor shortage had been through the importation of African slaves. At the time of the Louisiana Purchase, about half the people of the colony were black, and that ratio remained roughly the same until well after the Civil War. Congress ordered a halt to the foreign slave trade in 1804, but the smuggling of slaves continued on a fairly large scale for twenty years and to some extent for the remainder of the antebellum period.

Louisiana slaveholders seldom sold their human property voluntarily, but there were enough bankruptcies and forced sales to settle estates to afford buyers occasional opportunity to buy acclimated Negroes. However, most of the slaves bought by Louisiana purchasers came from the eastern seaboard or from Tennessee or Kentucky. The vast majority of bondsmen who entered Louisiana after the Louisiana Purchase accompanied immigrant masters, but the professional slave trader was an essential part of the slave economy. New Orleans was the greatest slave market in the country. The difference in value between workers on the worn soils of the Southeast and those employed on the rich new lands of Mississippi, Louisiana, and Texas almost assured the trader a profit. The slave trade was a cruel business, breaking up families and causing untold emotional agony. The term *being sold down the river* still connotes betrayal. On the other hand, the bondsman sold down the river or shipped to Louisiana from the East Coast was probably better off, in a material sense, than he had been in his former home. It is significant that, after the Civil War, black agricultural laborers moved voluntarily from the Southeast to the Southwest in numbers apparently equalling or excelling the number moved by migrating masters and slave traders before the war. To Louisiana's credit, it should be noted that her laws, alone among the

Southern states, forbade the selling of children under ten years of age away from their mothers.

Most of the work done by slaves was in the fields, raising sugar cane and cotton. It should be remembered that, although most slaveowners possessed fewer than ten slaves, most slaves were owned in groups of twenty or more. Those owned singly or in small groups worked side by side with their owners and performed practically all the tasks carried out on a small farm. On plantations, although there was more specialization, the vast majority were field hands. Among the specialists were artisans, house servants, drivers, and even a few Negro overseers. Drivers were the foremen of the plantation labor force, placed in charge of gangs doing some particular job. Most overseers were white men, though an exceptionally able slave might sometimes be assigned that duty; on most small and medium-sized plantations, the owner was his own overseer.

With rare exceptions, slaves were adequately fed, clothed, and housed according to the standards of the time. Corn meal and pork made up the basic ration, supplemented by fresh meat, fish, vegetables, white bread, and sugar when that was possible. The student of Louisiana slavery discovers few symptoms of diseases associated with malnutrition. The most repulsive practice, certainly not universal, was feeding slave children from troughs, as animals were fed. On large plantations the clothing issued to slaves might be almost military in its uniformity, but it was certainly adequate for Louisiana's mild climate. On small plantations and on farms, clothing purchased for the workers was often supplemented with hand-me-downs from the master's family; house servants seem more often than not to have worn garments given them by whites. Housing was not luxurious, and masters were careful to provide no closets, attics, or other places where stolen articles might be concealed, but most cabins were sufficient at the least to keep the occupants dry and warm. The small size of the cabins was not as much a hardship as might be assumed, because they were used mainly for sleeping. During the day slaves were out of doors at work.

The law recognized no legal marriage among slaves, but re-

cent students of slave life have concluded that black families
were surprisingly stable. A myth persists, encouraged by some
sensational fiction, that slave owners bred their bondsmen like
animals, but no historian has discovered an unquestionable in-
stance of such practices. Obviously owners wanted their blacks
to reproduce, because natural increase was one of the sources of
profit in slavery, and women were rewarded for bearing children
and taking good care of them. But in the Victorian nineteenth
century, most planters really seem to have been concerned with
encouraging Victorian morality, and they were probably wise;
that era was one of high birth rates for both white and black.
One unfortunate result of slavery was that the father had very
little responsibility for his children; the master and the mother
bore the burden. It has been suggested that this encouraged the
largely matriarchial family that developed among blacks in
Louisiana after slavery had come to an end.

Louisiana slaves were human beings, and recreation was a
necessity for them. Dancing was a favorite diversion, though it
was discouraged by some of the more puritanical churches.
Planters seem to have sponsored a feast and a dance more or
less consistently at Christmas and often at other times of the
year when the work was not heavy. Sometimes several planters
would combine forces for such a gala. Except on sugar plantations during the grinding, Sundays were almost without exception free from work, and it was not uncommon for a master to
let his people have Saturday afternoon for their own. When
slaves did work on Sunday, they were almost always paid for it;
some hired themselves out to a neighboring farmer in order to
accumulate a little money. The Fourth of July was commonly a
holiday, characterized by interminable patriotic speeches, but
Christmas week was the main holiday of the year.

On a sugar plantation, Christmas might be delayed until some
time in January, but it eventually came. In addition to enjoying
a feast and a dance, on Christmas morning the blacks trooped to
the master's house for gifts. These might be almost anything,
but it was a common practice to give the men a wool hat,
tobacco, and a drink of whiskey; women were likely to get a red
bandanna and perhaps a bright calico dress, and the children

could expect candy. After the distribution of gifts, adults often received passes for the remainder of the week so that they could visit neighboring plantations. Often, at Christmas and on Sundays, they gathered in the nearest town or hamlet; they were not welcome, but they gathered, anyway.

For slavery to exist, a rigid system of discipline was necessary. The fear of insurrection was never completely absent from the white population, and that fear was compounded by the fact that, in the plantation parishes, blacks outnumbered whites, sometimes more than ten to one. There was no doubt that an insurrection could be put down, but that would be little comfort to white families in the area where it took place. After 1811, there was no actual uprising, but abortive conspiracies and rumors were frequent enough to keep the fear very much alive. Perhaps the most effective preventive measure was the patrol, a group of men who traveled the roads at night, apprehending runaways and preventing surreptitious gatherings. All things considered, the methods used to prevent insurrection were remarkably effective. Even during the Civil War there were no real insurrections in Louisiana.

The French *Code Noir* was a rather lenient code, compared with slave laws in effect in some of the eastern seaboard states, and it remained the basic slave law of Louisiana until the late 1820s. Then, as awareness of the antislavery movement grew, the slave code became more and more harsh. A reading of the slave code can horrify, but it must be remembered that the law was intended to deal with the worst possible situation. In practice, its full rigor was invoked only when a black committed a crime that in some way threatened white supremacy. Murder or rape accomplished or attempted against a white—or even assault—was almost sure death for a slave. If whites did not take the law into their own hands, the courts could act almost as swiftly as a mob. It was not unusual for crime, trial, and execution to take place within one week.

For other crimes, the punishment of slaves was usually far less than the heaviest penalty provided by law. Imprisonment was rare, usually reserved for a black who had committed a crime against the person of a white under great provocation or for some incorrigible individual who had done nothing for which he could be legally executed. The difference between being confined at hard labor and being a plantation slave was not enough for imprisonment to be any great punishment. The black who stole, ran away, or assaulted a fellow slave was usually punished on the plantation. Such punishment might take many forms—some plantations had stocks such as were used in Puritan New England—but the lash was the most common instrument of correction. Masters who left records complained much about the pilfering habits of their human property, but so long as the slave ate what he stole, the master was not too greatly upset.

The most difficult problem in disciplining slaves was keeping them at work. Whether a black worked well or poorly had little or no effect on his own welfare or that of his family, so the economic motivation that kept the factory worker at his task did not exist. Some planters accomplished much with praise and rewards for good performance; *esprit de corps* was as possible with a field gang as with an infantry platoon. Another very important measure was a regular routine; the slave was much more likely to accomplish his task if he knew what was expected of him, and an accustomed routine provided that knowledge.

Such methods were limited, however. They had to be accompanied by sanctions to be invoked against those who did not deserve praise, who had no *esprit de corps,* who upset the established routine, or who ran away. On practically all plantations the whip provided that sanction. One should certainly not assume that on a well-run plantation all the slaves, or even very many of them, were lashed every day. On good days the whip was not used at all, though its presence in the hands of the overseer or driver was a constant reminder of its availability. Its prompt use on the person of the insubordinate, the shirker, or the otherwise delinquent kept the other hands at work. The fictional Simon Legree was not a typical master; but human nature being what it is, slaveowners included some men who could be compared with him. A slave was helpless against the master whose love of inflicting pain took precedence over his respect for public opinion and his desire for profit; but against the planter whose primary concern was making money, the slave did have some recourse. He could do as little work as possible; he could do his work poorly; he could spread disaffection; and as a last resort, he could run away.

When a Louisiana slave ran away, he was seldom attempting to achieve freedom. The obstacles between Louisiana and Canada were too many and too great. The ordinary runaway might be avoiding work, escaping punishment, or trying to get back to family and friends at a previous home. Some were chronic runaways who would have fled from responsibility had they been free men. Many, however, could be described with considerable accuracy as being on strike. Every day that a runaway was gone was a day's labor lost; it could never be regained. Discipline was a necessity for a slave regime, and it had to be strict, but a plantation work force had to be kept reasonably contented or the discontent was manifested in less cotton or less sugar produced.

Under French and Spanish law, emancipation of slaves had been fairly easy, but under American rule it became increasingly difficult. More and more obstacles were placed in the way of emancipation until, in 1857, the state's lawmakers forbade any emancipations whatsoever, and in 1859, apparently intoxicated by the exuberance of their own proslavery arguments, the legislators adopted a statute that permitted free Negroes to select a master and become slaves! This writer has found no evidence that any free person took advantage of that opportunity.

In the years before the Civil War, Louisiana was not a healthful place to live. No concept of sanitation existed, and with the sole exception of smallpox, no knowledge of immunization was available. Infant mortality was tragically high, mothers breathed a sigh of relief if their babies survived their second summer. Diarrhea, which killed by dehydration, was probably the most frequent cause of death for children, both black and white; but often they had been previously weakened by intestinal worms. Even when infants survived the crucial second summer, epidemics of diphtheria or whooping cough could be deadly. Tuberculosis, more often called "consumption," was not uncommon; it and pneumonia killed children and adults impartially. Blacks seem to have been somewhat more susceptible than whites to respiratory diseases.

On the other hand, perhaps because of some genetic heritage from Africa, Negroes seem to have been somewhat more resistant to fevers than were whites. Malaria was so common that it was almost taken for granted; no statistics are available, but it seems probable that only a fortunate few were able to go through life without at least one visitation of "chills and fever." Fortunately a specific cure for malaria—quinine—was known, so the disease brought death only when treatment was neglected. It was an enervating illness, however, and the use of quinine at best brought on constant ringing in the ears. Typhoid fever was endemic. It could hardly be otherwise when the need for sanitation was almost totally ignored. Probably as many Louisianians died of typhoid as of any other disease, but its toll was steady, year after year, and it did not attract the attention given to yellow fever and cholera. Despite the knowledge of vaccination, smallpox gathered its share of victims; it was particularly dreaded by women, because those who survived were often left with hideously pitted faces.

Yellow fever and cholera were the two most dreaded afflictions. Blacks contracted yellow fever, but they were much more likely to recover than were white victims. The malady was, of course, mosquito-borne and might break out at any time except in the dead of winter, though normally it began in late summer and continued until a frost put an end to the carriers. Apparently, the virus had to be reintroduced from the tropics before another epidemic could take place, because there were many years in which no cases were reported. The worst years, however, can only be described as deadly. Usually, though not always, the first outbreak was in New Orleans; newspapers would ignore early reports because of the adverse effect upon business, but soon the presence of the dreaded fever would be common knowledge. From New Orleans it would spread out over the city's trade routes, leaving death and debility in its wake.

Cholera did not afflict Louisiana so often as yellow fever, but when it did appear, it wreaked greater havoc. It was equally fatal to black and white, and when it reached the isolated people of a plantation, it might bring down two-thirds of them. In 1833 so many slaves died in the region of New Iberia that sugar planters were unable to harvest their crops; and in the national cholera epidemic of 1849–1850, 273 of the 376 slaves on Episcopal Bishop Leonidas Polk's plantation at Thibodaux had cholera, and 69 of them died. In New Orleans people died faster than they could be buried, and the stench of death hung over the city.

One reason for the deadliness of these and other diseases was that medical practice was almost as primitive as that of ancient Greece and Rome. Today, yellow fever and cholera can normally be treated successfully by rest and an abundance of liquids. Treatment in the nineteenth century was almost the opposite of what it should have been: massive doses of purgatives and emetics added to the dehydration that killed, and other medicines did more harm than good. A physicians's diary tells of the treatment of a slave: "Hill took cholera here last night, gave him 40 grains calomel, 20 grains gum camphor and 20 of Cayenne pepper, separated every hour with a grain of morphine twice. Mustard plasters on stomach and ankles and injections of camphor and laudanum. A sweat proper came out in three hours; he slept six hours. . . . Hill died the 5th.'' [2]

Under France and Spain, the Catholic Church had been the established church in Louisiana, but that favored position ended with the Louisiana Purchase. Soon after the purchase, the Vatican placed Louisiana under Bishop John Carrol of Baltimore, and in 1815 the entire Louisiana Purchase became the Diocese of Louisiana under Bishop Louis Dubourg. Louisiana was not oversupplied with priests; Dubourg reported at one time that there were only twelve in the entire province. Before a bishop had been appointed, Père Antoine de Sedella and Father Patrick Walsh had quarrelled over which of them was the rightful pastor of St. Louis Cathedral in New Orleans. The Catholics of New

2. R. F. McGuire Diary, April 1849, Department of Archives, Lousiana State University, Baton Rouge, La.

Orleans took sides in the dispute, and the quarrelling continued after Father Walsh's death. Père Antoine had hoped to be named bishop, and he apparently aroused his followers to oppose Bishop Dubourg. The latter was so disturbed by the prevailing factionalism that he moved his headquarters from New Orleans to the then frontier outpost of St. Louis in Missouri. Not until 1820 did the bishop again set foot in New Orleans, and not until 1823 did he move his residence there. Three years later Dubourg resigned his position in Louisiana and was appointed to a more peaceful diocese in France.

The next bishop of Louisiana was Leo Neckere, a man whose health was so poor that he was able to do little before his death in 1833. A strong hand was needed, because lay wardens were asserting control over the patronage and property of the church in many instances. The strength needed came with the appointment of Bishop Antoine Blanc to succeed Neckere. Bishop Blanc finally brought the wardens of St. Louis Cathedral to heel by withdrawing all clergy from services there, thus bringing pressure against his antagonists from those who wished to receive the sacraments. The wardens carried their case to the Louisiana supreme court and also tried to get legislation passed confirming their position, but the bishop was victorious at every turn. By 1844 the wardens had been subdued in church, court, and legislature. In recognition of his achievements, Blanc was named head of a new Archbishopric of Louisiana with dioceses at New Orleans and Natchitoches. By 1860 there were ninety-nine Catholic churches in the state.

Some Protestants had come to Louisiana before 1803, but it was then illegal for them to hold public worship. Joseph Willis, a free mulatto from South Carolina, is usually recognized as the founder of the Baptist Church in Louisiana as a result of evangelism in the Opelousas region in 1804. The first Methodist congregation was established in the same area, two years later. An Episcopal church had been organized in New Orleans in 1805, a Methodist church by 1813, and a Presbyterian church by 1817. A Jewish congregation became active in 1828. Some Protestant religious leaders were Theodore Clapp, Presbyterian-turned-Unitarian, whose heresy trial attracted national attention;

Leonidas Polk, first Episcopal Bishop of Louisiana, later to die on the battlefield as a Confederate general; and Benjamin M. Palmer, a Presbyterian. Protestant growth in Louisiana was not rapid until after 1840, but by 1860, as more and more immigrants from the Southeast moved in, there were reported to be 199 Methodist, 161 Baptist, 42 Presbyterian, and 33 Episcopal churches.

French and Spanish laws requiring that slaves be baptized into the Catholic Church were often disregarded, and it was not until about 1840 that a serious Protestant effort to evangelize slaves began. The degree to which this effort was successful cannot be determined, but the number of black members of existing Protestant churches certainly did increase. In the plantation regions it was not at all unusual for a church to have more black than white members, though they definitely held an inferior position in the congregation. If given a choice, blacks preferred the enthusiasm of Methodist or Baptist services to the ritualism of the Roman Catholic or Episcopalian or the intellectual puritanism of the Presbyterian. Since they often had no option except to belong to the church to which their masters belonged, however, many were Catholics, Episcopalians, or Presbyterians. One of the first assertions of black freedom after emancipation was to leave these churches and flock into various Baptist and Methodist sects. Some traces of African religious practices persisted, and still persist, but the vast majority of Louisiana blacks enthusiastically accepted Christianity as their religion.

Although the state constitution adopted in 1845 called for state support of education, and although the legislature adopted statutes providing for a system of public schools, no real public school system was established in Louisiana outside the city of New Orleans, and the New Orleans system was a creation of the city rather than the state. Public schools were opposed by planters, who felt with some justification that they would have to pay for them, and by the Catholic Church, which feared secularism. Catholic parochial schools were available in many parishes and were becoming more numerous with the passage of time. A few of the more wealthy planters employed tutors, but the vast majority of Protestant children who attended school went to a private school, often with a faculty of one or two teachers. Many such schools could almost be termed Protestant parochial schools, because they were taught by Protestant clergymen to supplement their meager incomes.

Among real institutions of higher learning was the Medical College of Louisiana, established in 1834 and renamed the University of Louisiana by the Constitution of 1845. It would eventually become Tulane University. Centenary College has been nomadic. Founded at Jackson, Louisiana, in 1825, it was moved to Mississippi, then back to Jackson in 1845, then to Shreveport in 1908. In 1860 the Louisiana State Seminary of Learning and Military Academy was established at Alexandria with Colonel William Tecumseh Sherman, later to carry fire and sword through the South, as its first superintendent. The school was closed during the Civil War, reopened afterward, and became Louisiana State University after a fire on the original campus forced removal to Baton Rouge.

Because New Orleans was a large city, at one time or another before the Civil War at least eighteen newspapers were published there in French, English, German, or Spanish. Antebellum newspapers served as vehicles for the ideas of their editors, and news was secondary to editorial content. Readers may have remained ignorant of events in Tasmania or Southeast Asia, but they were well informed about the editor's position on politics, economics, and the social questions of the day. So long as they did not impugn the reputation of a man zealous to defend his honor or contradict the southern position on the slavery issue, editors seem to have been free to take any point of view that appealed to them.

Antebellum Louisiana was certainly not a cultural oasis in a southern desert of proslavery oratory, but since it did boast a cosmopolitan metropolis, it had cultural features lacking in most of the South. That was particularly true of the theater; drama in French and in English was regular fare in New Orleans. Practically every great name in nineteenth-century drama and opera appeared there sooner or later, some of them many times. The St. Charles Theater was nationally famous.

Louisiana literature might have been more noteworthy had the state not been bilingual, though that is not necessarily true. Two important periodicals appeared in New Orleans, the short-lived *Southern Quarterly Review* and the more enduring *De Bow's Review*. J. D. B. De Bow was primarily concerned with advancing southern agriculture, but he printed essays on almost any subject, making his publication essential source material for any serious study of southern history. Theodore O'Hara was probably the best antebellum poet. *Les Cenelles,* a book of poems by black Louisiana authors, was published in 1845, but the volume is more noteworthy for its origins than for its verse. Louisiana's greatest literary contribution was in the field of history. François Xavier Martin published a one-volume history of Louisiana, and Charles Gayarré penned the history of the colony and state in a four-volume work, eventually published in both French and English. Considering that much of the state was still frontier, that most of the best minds of the state were occupied with religion or the defense of slavery or both, and that the audience for works in French was strictly limited, Louisiana's literary production during the antebellum period is creditable. The last third of the nineteenth century compares poorly with prewar years; George Washington Cable was probably a better writer than any of his antebellum predecessors, but he was very much alone.

Politics in antebellum Louisiana went through several distinct periods, but in every phase the state was controlled by a combination of planters and New Orleans businessmen. Such so-called government by gentlemen began under France and Spain, continued during the territorial period, and was reinforced by the adoption in 1812 of a modified version of the aristocratic Kentucky state constitution as Louisiana's basic law. The dominance of the planter-businessman alliance in government continued throughout the antebellum period and, except for the interruption of Reconstruction, for two generations after secession.

The Federalist party was declining when Louisiana came into the Union, and it had almost no adherents in the new state, because Federalists in Congress had opposed admission. During the first decade of statehood, Louisiana political conflict was largely Anglo-American versus Latin, but by the 1830s, national politics had begun to affect politics in the Pelican State. When the Jeffersonian Republicans divided into National Republicans on the one hand and Jacksonian Democrats on the other, Louisianians divided also. In general, the Florida Parishes and North Louisiana followed Jackson, while South Louisiana favored National Republicans in general and Henry Clay in particular; so in a sense the division was a continuation of the Anglo-versus-Latin alignment. The National Republicans were successful more often than not in early state contests, but Andrew Jackson carried the state in the presidential contests of 1828 and 1832.

By the middle 1830s, the term *National Republican* was no longer heard; the Whig Party became the opposition to the Jacksonians, who had come to be called simply Democrats. Louisiana politics has never been simple, and any description of party alignments is necessarily oversimplified, perhaps grossly oversimplified. In general, however, South Louisiana, where sugar planters were dependent upon a protective tariff to compete with sugar imported from abroad, tended to favor the pro-tariff Whigs. North Louisiana and the Florida Parishes, which produced cotton to be sold in a free world market, favored the antitariff Democrats. But it must not be thought that economic interests alone dictated party loyalties. The Anglo-American community of New Orleans tended to be Whig; people of Latin ancestry, even the upper classes, voted Democratic. The New Orleans Democratic vote was swelled during the 1840s by the arrival of thousands of Irish and German immigrants. At the same time, however, the Whig vote was growing among the cotton planters of the Florida Parishes and of the alluvial parishes along the Mississippi River as they became more wealthy. If such an account seems confusing, it is because party alignment in antebellum Louisiana *was* confusing.

Probably Louisiana politics can be better understood if set forth in other than party terms. Certain more or less persistent conflicting interests have characterized the state's political activity for most of its history. One might list Protestant versus Catholic, North Louisiana versus South Louisiana, Anglo versus Latin, sugar versus cotton, city versus country, and planter versus farmer. Except that farmers as a class have almost ceased to exist, these conflicts are still apparent in Louisiana politics today. For example, Governor Edwin Edwards, first elected in 1972—a man of Acadian ancestry, despite his Anglo-Saxon name—is the first Catholic to win that office in the twentieth century and the first South Louisianian from anywhere other than New Orleans to do so since 1908.

In 1845 a constitutional convention was called by the Democratic legislature to provide a government more responsive to the popular will and more in accord with the accepted principles of Jacksonian democracy. The election of delegates, however, gave the conservative Whigs almost as great a representation as the Democrats, and some of the Democrats were equally conservative. The convention did abolish all property qualifications for voting and holding office, make most local offices elective, and require that judges, who had previously been appointed for life, serve fixed terms. But the constitution definitely did not put control of state government into popular hands. The significant battle in the convention was fought over the apportionment of representation in the legislature. As compromised, the parishes were to be represented in the lower house in proportion to the number of registered voters, but apportionment for the state senate was according to total population, black and white. Thus a parish dominated by a few great planters and containing a large number of voteless slaves would have the same representation in the senate as a parish populated by an equal number of free men. Thus the dominant planter class had at the least a veto over any legislation it opposed. Another constitution was adopted in 1852, under which apportionment in both houses was based on total population. Any tendency toward more democracy in antebellum Louisiana could most accurately be described as more apparent than real.

Slavery was never an internal issue in Louisiana politics; all factions agreed that African servitude was right and that those who opposed it were fanatic bigots or radical subversives, or both. The stronger the attacks upon slavery from the North, the more self-righteous did the Louisiana politician become in his defense of it. Nonetheless, as the question came more and more to occupy center stage in national politics, it was inevitable that it should have an effect upon politics within Louisiana. The slavery dispute destroyed the Whig party, because large numbers of Northern Whigs were at least opposed to the expansion of slavery, and many Southern Whigs of the planter class agreed fully with their Democratic counterparts that the expansion of slavery was essential to its survival. In 1856 many former Whigs cast their lot with the Native American or "Know-Nothing" party, a nativist, antiforeign and anti-Catholic organization that came into being largely as a reaction to the massive Irish and German immigration of the 1840s and 1850s. In Louisiana, that meant that some Catholics supported an anti-Catholic party, though most of the state's Know-Nothings seem to have been New Orleans Anglo-Americans. The Know-Nothings succeeded in dominating New Orleans politics for a season, but statewide they were never a serious threat to the Democrats.

The dominant Democrats did divide into factions, one led by John Slidell, the other by Pierre Soulé. Basically, however, what caused that division was a conflict of personalities, not a disagreement over political principles. At the time of the Compromise of 1850, Soulé was a secessionist, Slidell a Unionist. Ten years later Slidell had reversed his position, and Soulé became, though hardly a Unionist, certainly an opponent of a separate southern Democratic party. Slidell, Soulé, and old Whigs alike were committed to the defense of slavery, and all but a very few leaders agreed that secession was the legitimate and appropriate means of defense; there might be disagreement over necessity and timing, but on propriety and right there was agreement. What is truly remarkable is that the majority of slaveless farmers rallied behind the planters to prevent any interference with slavery. They consented to government by gentlemen, and when the policies of their gentlemen leaders put them on the road that would bring destruction upon antebellum Louisiana, they followed without question.

6

Rush to Destruction:
Louisiana and the Civil War

GIVEN the hindsight afforded by more than a century, it is difficult to justify Louisiana's attempted secession from the Union on any basis of self-interest. The state's dominant merchant-planter class prospered under the antebellum regime, and during the 1850s it was prospering more than ever before. The prosperity of sugar planters depended upon protection from foreign sugar imports, and the other seceding states were known to be opposed in principle to a protective tariff. New Orleans drew a significant part of its trade from the free states of the upper Mississippi valley, and that trade certainly could not be expected to continue unchanged, even if secession could be carried out peacefully. Furthermore, without access by sea to the markets of the North and the rest of the world, New Orleans was sure to face economic strangulation, and in case of war the superiority of the Union navy was almost certain to deny such access. Finally, New Orleans's location on the Mississippi made it vulnerable to Union naval attack downriver from the North or upriver from the Gulf of Mexico.

Despite the obfuscation of speeches on states' rights and other overfervent nationalistic rhetoric, Louisiana and the South seceded from the Union primarily because secession was felt to be necessary to preserve Negro slavery. As it happened, however, the war brought on by secession destroyed slavery, which otherwise might have endured indefinitely. President Lincoln, as he recognized, had no power to interfere with slavery in the states where it already existed, and it is difficult to see what might have brought it to an end before the mechanization of southern agriculture in the mid-twentieth century. It might even be said that the existence of slavery could have delayed or prevented mechanization, and even if agricultural machinery had ended gang labor in the fields, it is possible that domestic servitude might have continued for years longer. Most Louisianians in 1860 and 1861 were ruled by rhetoric and passion, however, not by reason; Louisiana did secede, the war was fought, and chattel slavery was ended. In truth, the condition of Louisiana blacks was not appreciably improved, but the position of the state's whites was immeasurably worsened, and all this at a cost in blood greater than Louisiana has paid in any other war.

Southern statesmen, Louisiana's among them, had been proclaiming loudly for four years that secession would follow the election of a Republican to the presidency. It is possible that that was a self-fulfilling prophecy. The South had insisted that it would secede if a Republican was elected; when a Republican was elected, the South had a choice of seceding or eating its words. After the Democrats split into two factions, no one in Louisiana favored Lincoln, but many Know-Nothings and old Whigs wanted neither Northern nor Southern Democrat. These men rallied enthusiastically behind John Bell of Tennessee, the candidate of the Constitutional Union party, created in an effort to avoid disunion. Southern Democrat John C. Breckenridge had a plurality of the votes cast in Louisiana and therefore received the state's electoral vote, but it is significant that the vote for Stephen A. Douglas and Bell combined exceeded that cast for Breckenridge. In November of 1860, almost surely, a majority of those who went to the polls in Louisiana were opposed to secession.

That majority opposition would not last long. Following the secession of South Carolina, a wave of enthusiasm rolled over the lower South, including Louisiana. One public figure after another announced his support for secession; those who opposed withdrawal from the Union soon found it inadvisable to speak out openly. Rather than directly opposing secession, they advocated "co-operation," that is, waiting until the slave states could meet together, decide what to do, and then act in unison. When the legislature called for the election of delegates to a convention that would decide for or against secession, no overt Unionists were candidates. On the contrary, where there were contests, they were between co-operationists on the one hand and immediate secessionists on the other.

Because the attitudes of many of the candidates were uncertain, historians have difficulty in deciding how great a majority in the secession election of January 1861 favored secession, or even whether a majority favored secession at all. Certainly there was a strong tide of public opinion in favor of secession flowing from the time of the presidential election of 1860 until the convention acted, on January 26, 1861, to take Louisiana out of the Union. Sentiment in the convention was so overwhelmingly secessionist that only a handful of those opposed dared refuse to sign the ordinance of secession after it had been adopted.

Delegates were sent by the convention to Montgomery, Alabama, where a constitution was being drawn up for the Confederate States of America. Within Louisiana Federal posts had been taken over by state authorities even before secession had been accomplished. Finally, the Louisiana convention voted to establish state military forces, some of which had already been organized, and it was understood that these would be transferred to the authority of the Confederate government when it had come into being. Patriotic speeches, colorful uniforms, the presentation of flags by ladies, and a general glow of Southern patriotism were probably necessary to develop fighting spirit for the war that wise men knew lay ahead. On March 21, 1861, Louisiana officially became one of the Confederate States of America.

There was an exceptionally gala Mardi Gras that year; speeches, band music, the recruitment of unarmed men, and drilling by officers whose ignorance of drill was matched only by that of their men went on almost incessantly. By the end of June 1861, sixteen thousand men were enlisted, and seventy-

four hundred were already in Confederate service. At Camp
Moore, on the Amite River, four thousand more were receiving
sketchy training, and thousands of others were impatiently waiting to be armed. It was noteworthy even in the beginning, however, that the plantation parishes were much more ardent in their
desire to defend the South than were the yeoman farmers of the
hills or the Acadians of the Attakapas Region. Nonetheless,
before the end of the year, more than sixteen thousand men had
been sent out of the state. Throughout the war, about fifty-six
thousand Louisianians were mustered into service, many of
them "volunteers" who enlisted to escape being drafted after a
Conscription Act was adopted in 1862.

Some Louisianians took part in the First Battle of Manassas
in June of 1861, but it was not until the bloody two days of
Shiloh, in early April 1862, that the reality of war was brought
home to the state. For two weeks after the battle, trains arrived
in New Orleans carrying dead and wounded from that battlefield, including the corpse of Albert Sidney Johnston, the Confederate commander. But the people of New Orleans would not
have long to dwell upon Confederate defeat in Tennessee, because Commodore David Farragut was threatening New Orleans
itself with a naval force based in the Gulf.

The Federal blockade of the Gulf Coast had gained effec-
tiveness before the end of 1861, and in February Farragut had
arrived to take command of an attack upon New Orleans.
Troops under Major General Benjamin F. Butler would occupy
the city after it fell. New Orleans itself was virtually defenseless, and the Confederate commander, General Mansfield Lovell, relied upon Forts St. Philip and Jackson, on the banks of the
Mississippi well below the city, and upon a hastily assembled
and disorganized fleet of river boats and naval craft. One huge
ironclad, the *Louisiana,* was under construction and might have
made a difference in the battle, had its engines been in working
order, but no "might have been" has ever changed history.

Farragut began with a bombardment of the forts, but after
five days of shelling, the morale of the garrisons had been dam-
aged far more than the forts themselves, and the commodore,
who had never believed that the battle could be won easily,

prepared to force his way past the Confederate guns. That he did in the early morning hours of April 24. The battle was a confused melee, almost a case of every ship for itself; but when it was over, all but a few of the Union ships were safely past the forts that now could be left for the army to reduce. Indeed, once the Union fleet had passed, the forts served no useful purpose, and the men of the garrisons were aware of that. On the night of April 27, surrounded by Union troops, the men of Fort Jackson mutinied and began spiking their guns. The next day both forts were surrendered.

After passing the forts and defeating the mismanaged Confederate river fleet, including the incomplete *Louisiana,* Farragut proceeded upriver to his objective. The river was high, the surface of the water being well above the level of the streets behind the levee. Thus the guns of the Union fleet looked menacingly down upon the city. What Confederate General Lovell could not carry away, he destroyed or left to the mercy of the mob, which quickly disposed of practically everything drinkable or eatable.

On April 25 when Farragut demanded that Mayor John T. Monroe surrender the city, Monroe argued that he could not, because New Orleans was under martial law. In fact, the two officers who went ashore were in real danger from a mob frustrated by defeat and fortified by liquor. Quibbling by the city officials could not last long in the face of Union power, and with the arrival of Butler's troops on May 1, 1862, New Orleans became an occupied city for the remainder of the war.

Butler's tenure as commander in New Orleans did not extend past late 1862, but his is still probably the most hated name in Louisiana history. Part of the reason was simply that he represented the conqueror. His appearance was against him, as well: he was corpulent; one of his eyes did not track with the other; and his disposition does not seem to have been a lovable one. Before he departed, there was an odor of corruption about his headquarters; whether Butler himself was implicated in trade with the enemy is still uncertain, but there is no doubt that his brother made a tidy fortune in such trade. A major reason why Butler was so hated, however, was that he treated the people of New Orleans as a conquered people who would have welcomed a Confederate army or a pestilence that would have rid them of the Union army. He was quite correct in this estimation of the people's attitude. Parenthetically, in order to create work for the unemployed and to protect his troops from disease, Butler gave New Orleans the first thorough physical cleaning that it had had in its existence; no serious yellow fever or cholera epidemic broke out until 1867, when the place had again become filthy.

The single act of Butler's that won him most opprobrium, at home and abroad, was his "woman order." The men of the Crescent City were quickly brought to outward form of good behavior, but the women—most of them lower class but some of them not—made a practice of abusing Federal officers and men verbally, and in some cases spitting upon them. Butler's solution was to proclaim that any woman who engaged in such behavior would be treated as a prostitute plying her trade. The Victorian world recoiled in horror, but Union troops were seldom insulted again so long as Butler commanded the occupation. The ladies reportedly achieved revenge by placing Butler's portrait in the bottom of their chamber pots.

By the end of 1862, Vicksburg in Mississippi and Port Hudson in Louisiana were the only important places on the Mississippi River still in Confederate hands. After failing to take Vicksburg in 1862, Union forces under General Ulysses S. Grant encamped on the Louisiana side of the river. In the spring of 1863, as the roads dried, Grant moved his troops south, down the west bank of the river, while gunboats and transports ran the guns of Vicksburg. He crossed the river into Mississippi; then, living off the country, marched to Jackson, thence back to Vicksburg, which he invested and eventually forced to surrender. The right bank of the Mississippi from the Arkansas line down to Vidalia, opposite Natchez, was thus tenuously occupied by Union forces.

While Grant was attacking Vicksburg, General Nathaniel P. Banks, who had replaced Butler in command of occupied South Louisiana, led his forces against Port Hudson. The Union commander tried two assaults, both of which were repulsed with great loss; it should be mentioned that black Louisianians, serving in the Union army, fought with great gallantry in these at-

tacks. Banks should not be blamed unduly for the bloody re-
pulses he suffered. Grant and Robert E. Lee still had not
comprehended the fact that the rifle and the artillery in use in
the Civil War made it possible for a small force in a strong position to repulse a much larger one attacking in the open. Union
losses at Port Hudson were not comparable to Lee's on the third
day at Gettysburg or Grant's in his assaults at Vicksburg or, a
year later, at Cold Harbor. Banks had surrounded Port Hudson,
and the results that military action could not achieve quickly
starvation would achieve slowly. The Confederate commander
eventually surrendered when he learned that Vicksburg had
fallen, but he could not have held out much longer, in any case.
The fall of Vicksburg and Port Hudson gave the Union control
of the Mississippi from its source to the Gulf of Mexico. The
Confederacy was split into two parts. As for Louisiana, although a few bands of Confederate troops remained in the
Florida Parishes, basically only north-central and northwestern
Louisiana remained in Confederate control.

In 1864, General Banks sought to win control of the remainder of Louisiana by driving up the Red River to Shreveport
and thence into Texas. Had this expedition succeeded, almost
all of Louisiana would have come under Federal control, but
Banks's luck had run out. Accompanied by naval gunboats and
transports, he proceeded up the Red River to Alexandria, then
pushed on to Natchitoches. The opposing Confederate commander, General Richard Taylor, son of President Zachary Taylor, retreated before the Union advance. So long as the Union
army kept close to the Red River, Taylor was most reluctant to
give battle. There is no evidence that gunboat fire was any more
effective than artillery fire during the Civil War, but its effect
upon the minds of Confederate soldiers was devastating. Men
who would advance into a storm of field-artillery fire would take
to their heels as soon as a gunboat began to lob shells among
them or even toward them.

When he left Natchitoches, Banks did not take secondary
roads that would have kept him near the Red River: he took a
shorter route leading through Pleasant Hill to Mansfield, taking
him many miles from naval support. Taylor decided to make a

stand at Mansfield, and there on April 8, 1864, he inflicted a sharp defeat upon Banks, who lost more than two thousand men killed, wounded, or captured. At the end of the battle, Banks still had decided numerical superiority, and most of his men were still full of fight, but the general's morale had been shattered. Knowing that Taylor would follow up his victory, Banks drew up defensive lines at Pleasant Hill, and there on April 9 he repulsed the Confederates. Probably he could have resumed his advance, but instead he ordered a retreat. The Union forces returned to New Orleans, where some units were transferred to the east.

In addition to these major campaigns, lesser expeditions, raids, and counterraids were going on from 1862 until the war finally ended. Northern thrusts went into the Felicianas, up the Jackson Railroad to the Ponchatoula area, westward along the railroad to the Atchafalaya and then onward up Bayou Teche to Franklin, New Iberia, and northward to Opelousas. Confederates consistently raided the rich plantation region along the Mississippi north of the Red, the Baton Rouge area, and the west bank of the Mississippi as far south as Donaldsonville and Boutte. Thus the campaigning was over the most fertile and prosperous areas of the state. It mattered little whether the land was trodden by Confederate or Union armies. Union forces destroyed property, including buildings, indiscriminately in taking vengeance upon their foes and attempting to destroy the South's ability to wage war; Banks's march up and down the Red River was probably as destructive to the property in his path as was Sherman's march across Georgia. But at least Union troops were normally well supplied. The Confederate armies of necessity lived off the land, and their passage left nothing edible behind. It was to be years before the land itself recovered from the ravages of the war.

In traversing the more fertile regions of Louisiana, the northern armies went into those areas of the greatest slave population. In every case, hundreds and thousands of blacks followed the men in blue, leaving their onetime owners infuriated but helpless. It should be added that thousands of others, for one reason or another, decided not to leave their homes, but refused to work as hard or as long as they had worked before the war. Once again, owners and overseers might be infuriated, but there was little that they could do. Tens of thousands of blacks gathered in "contraband camps" at Vicksburg and New Orleans. Coming from an isolated plantation environment, these people were unusually subject to communicable diseases; that, combined with lack of sanitation, brought terribly high death rates to the camps, but still the former slaves came, refuting the arguments of those who had maintained that slavery in the South was a beneficent institution and that the slaves were happier than they could be in any other condition.

The fact that black troops fought well at Port Hudson has already been mentioned. The recruitment of Negro troops in Louisiana began, somewhat unofficially, under General Butler, but by 1863 large numbers of blacks were being enlisted in the Union army. It is estimated that some two hundred thousand served in all, but it is impossible to say how many of them came from Louisiana. Before the end of the war, Negroes were in effect being impressed by soldiers who went into the countryside and took them from the fields where they were working, then put them in uniform. Some fought well, some fought poorly, but the demand for their services was increasing as the war came to an end. Also it is worth noting that, after the North had demonstrated that blacks could be soldiers, some of the ablest men in the South, including Robert E. Lee, advocated enlisting them in the Confederate army.

Blacks were not the only Louisianians who failed to support the Confederate cause. There had been men opposed to secession from the beginning, though most of them at least gave lip service to the Confederacy once war had begun. After the fall of New Orleans, many there gladly took the oath of allegiance to the Union. It is uncertain how deeply the widely celebrated enthusiasm for secession and war that existed in 1861 penetrated among the people of the rural parishes, but it had greatly diminished by the end of 1862.

There were many causes for discontent. The Confederate conscription act of 1862 discriminated against poorer people. There were many exemptions, the most unpopular one being one man exempt for each twenty slaves on a plantation. This "twenty-nigger law" aroused much bitterness among the slaveless farmers of north and south Louisiana. Likewise, the fact that a wealthy man could buy a substitute galled the poor, who had no money for such a purpose. The Confederate tax in kind on farm produce gave no joy to any farmer, but the poor family was less likely to be able to spare the foodstuffs taken by the tax collector. With considerable justice, the yeoman farmer and the poor white complained that the struggle was "a rich man's war and a poor man's fight." But probably the most potent factor in breeding discontent was the fact that after the fall of New Orleans nothing that happened in Louisiana brought encouragement to Confederate hopes until Banks's defeat in 1864, and by then it took no genius to see that the prospects of the Confederacy were poor everywhere.

The general discontent manifested itself first in desertions. Louisiana soldiers began to desert after Shiloh, and after the fall of Vicksburg and Port Hudson the number of desertions increased greatly. Many deserters were caught and shot, but for each one so punished, perhaps a hundred made good their escape. By 1864 hardship at home was a definite factor in encouraging desertion; it was hard for a conscript to resist a plea from his wife that he come home to keep his children from starving. Kirby Smith's troops in the Trans-Mississippi, not all of them Louisianians, deserted in such numbers that five or ten were executed each Friday in an attempt to frighten the remainder into staying at their posts, but to no avail.

A man could not desert, of course, unless he had volunteered or been conscripted into the army. More and more, as the war continued, men refused to volunteer and took to the woods and swamps when conscription bands appeared in the neighborhood. Most such men simply made themselves a lean-to or dugout in the nearby woods or swamps where they could take refuge. They worked their fields as well as they could and looked after whatever animals they possessed. How many there were, we do not know. Records were not kept, but there were seemingly such men in every Confederate-controlled parish in the state; certainly there were thousands of them, and there may have been ten thousand. It would not be correct to say that these men were pro-Union or even anti-Confederate; basically, they were opposed to a war in which they had nothing to gain and much, including their lives, to lose.

Deserters from both armies, draft-dodgers, and sometimes runaway slaves often formed into bands known as jayhawkers. These outlaws were especially prevalent in the areas not firmly controlled by either army. Some raided isolated homesteads and even army posts of both sides impartially, simply to obtain the wherewithal to stay alive. Others seem to have been outright brigands, robbing, raping, and murdering as they pleased, and growing more cruel and merciless as they became more accustomed to a lawless life. They were found almost everywhere in the state. One group based itself in the Atchafalaya swamp, where it could raid westward to the Teche region and eastward to Bayou Lafourche. A Union officer at Thibodaux said, in frustration: "If we pursue them with cavalry, they take to their canoes and small boats. If we undertake to cut them off with a gunboat, they run into a chain of smaller bayous where a gunboat cannot follow them." [1] In St. Landry Parish a group of jayhawkers defeated the first Confederate force sent against it but later was scattered by a stronger expedition. Another gang in Madison Parish was led by a huge black man. When the depredations of these outlaws were added to the destruction wreaked by troops of both sides, the damage to Louisiana was significantly increased.

Other than the bravery of her sons in Virginia and Tennessee and in countless battles and skirmishes throughout the war years, Louisiana had little to boast of in regard to the Civil War. However, Henry Watkins Allen, who was elected governor in autumn of 1863 and took office in January of 1864, was a man of whom any state or nation could be proud. Allen, a native Virginian, had emigrated westward and eventually settled on a sugar plantation on the west side of the Mississippi, north of Baton Rouge. He fought in the Texas War of Independence,

1. Quoted in Ethel Taylor, "Discontent in Confederate Louisiana," *Louisiana History* 2 (1961):427.

early became an officer in the Confederate army, and was shot
through the cheek at Shiloh. In the Battle of Baton Rouge his
legs were grievously mangled by an exploding artillery shell
that killed his horse. Afterward he was promoted to the rank of
brigadier general, but he was never again able to walk without
crutches. In 1863, although he made no effort to campaign, he
was elected governor of Louisiana by an overwhelming margin.
Despite his physical condition, before taking office he made a
tour and saw at first hand the condition of that part of the state
that remained in Confederate control; he formed some definite
ideas about what should be done to improve the lot of the people.

Allen found that, in the midst of one of the greatest cotton-
producing areas in the world, people were almost naked, that
medicines were in particularly short supply, and that the families of men in the service were suffering greatly. His accomplishments in a year and a half of office in solving these
problems while at the same time giving all the support possible
to the military effort can only be described as remarkable. In
fairness to governors of states farther east, it must be pointed
out that Allen had a trade route to Mexico available across
Texas, something not available to other state magistrates. He
took full advantage of this situation and, in the name of the state
of Louisiana, carried on a brisk trade in cotton with blockade
runners in Galveston and, more especially, traders across the
Rio Grande River from Brownsville, Texas. He strongly opposed the effort of General Kirby Smith to destroy all the cotton
in Louisiana to prevent its falling into Union hands. The earnings from this cotton trade went to buy cotton cards necessary to
prepare cotton for spinning, and to buy medicines, newsprint,
and other needed civilian supplies as well as military goods.

Trade from abroad could not begin to supply all Louisiana's
needs, so Allen turned to what might be called a form of state
socialism. State-owned factories were set up to produce cotton
cards so that women could once more manufacture cloth at
home, and before the end of the war two cloth-making factories
and one rope walk were in operation. The governor also established a "laboratory" for the manufacture of medicines in

the buildings of an old school at Mt. Lebanon, and a state dispensary and a state store were established at Shreveport. The laboratory was quickly producing all the medicinal alcohol and turpentine needed, as well as a number of medicines made from native plants, including castor oil, which may or may not have been useful. At the least they may have been comforting.

At Allen's urging, the legislature provided pensions for widows of men dead in Confederate service, for those impoverished by the absence of a husband or father, and for wounded veterans. He even sought to provide relief supplies for prisoners in Northern prison camps, though this accomplished little. Louisiana had no iron ore, so Allen bought for the state a quarter interest in iron works in Texas, then took over a foundry in Shreveport to use the iron. By the spring of 1865, the foundry was in full operation. Likewise, Allen took over control of salt manufacture and distribution, salt being one of the necessities most difficult to obtain in the Confederacy. His efforts not only improved the lot of the people of Confederate Louisiana; they were also profitable, returning some \$2 million to the treasury from the dispensary alone. But of course it was all in vain; just when the governor's program was beginning to bring results, military defeat brought an end to the Confederacy. Even in defeat, however, Allen served the people of Louisiana. He ordered all the goods in the state store put on sale for state, not Confederate, currency, giving some worth to this paper to the last possible moment. Allen expatriated himself and died soon afterward in Mexico City.

Louisiana had provided a total of about fifty-six thousand men for the Confederacy, and about eleven thousand of them had died of wounds or disease. Probably as many more were maimed to some degree. While the young white men of the state were being killed and crippled under the Confederate flag, thousands of young black men from Louisiana were suffering the same fate under the Stars and Stripes. It can be assumed that in the Civil War, as in most wars, it was the best young men who fell. It was most significant that so large a proportion of the laboring force of the most productive age was lost. Not measurable, but almost certainly more significant, was the loss of future leadership. That lack of leadership was to plague the state for two generations, almost two-thirds of a century, in politics, and surely it can be assumed that economic leadership also was crippled.

The destruction of men combined with the destruction of property to leave the state, rich in many respects before the Civil War, a land of poverty in the generations that followed. In the years to come Radical Republicans would blame poverty upon Rebels, Bourbon Democrats would blame it upon Radical Republicans, Populists would blame it upon big business, and others would blame such varied things as hookworm, malaria, lack of education, economic colonialism, and the large number of blacks in the population. There was an element of plausibility in most such accusations, but they all missed the main point. Louisiana was left impoverished because she had been on the losing side in the first total war in history, a war involving the greater part of the population and resources of the nation. She had lost the men and the capital necessary to retain or achieve prosperity. The years have given an element of glory to the "lost cause," and the courage of the men who fought on both sides was glorious, but the statues of Confederate soldiers that stand facing north on the courthouse grounds of most parish seats in Louisiana are grim of countenance. Well they might be, because the men they represent engaged in and lost a grim struggle. Perhaps it was worth it to end slavery, but that makes the story even more tragic, since white Louisianians were fighting to save slavery.

7

Crusaders and Crooks:
Political Reconstruction

$\mathcal{L}$OUISIANA'S folk memory of the eleven years after the Confederacy went down in defeat is more harrowing than the memory of the Civil War itself. That folk memory, however, was largely formed by Bourbon politicians promoting their own interests, and it lacks much in accuracy. Men and women who lived through Reconstruction were far more interested in making a living, keeping their health and their families, and getting along with their neighbors than in joining the struggle between Radical Republican and conservative Democrat. For a generation or more after political Reconstruction was over, however, the politicians cultivated their myth of horror, to avoid the necessity of dealing with real social and economic issues. Paradoxically, white Louisianians who were on the losing side in the bloody American Civil War remember it as a glorious struggle. The battle of political Reconstruction they won, but they remember those years as the worst in their history.

Reconstruction after the Civil War is one of the most controversial eras in American history, and events in Louisiana are certainly as controversial as any others. One school of historians sees nothing good in the postwar treatment of the South, only vengeance taken upon a helpless people by a vindictive North. Others see Reconstruction as the means whereby the Republican party kept itself in power nationally, an object so important to the party's leaders that it justified any necessary repression of the white South. To some it was a bacchanalia of political and financial corruption made possible by the unwise giving of political equality to black people barely removed from slavery and not ready for the responsibilities of citizenship. Others have seen northern manufacturing interests protecting themselves against the revival of free-trade sentiment in Congress and insuring the continuation of federal subsidies to business corporations. A few Marxists have seen either a progressive step from feudalism to capitalism on the road to socialism or a premature proletarian revolt against capitalism. Still another group of historians interprets Reconstruction as an abortive but real effort to assure the political rights and, to some extent, all civil rights of black people. These various interpretations are not all mutually exclusive, of course, but none of them, and perhaps not all of them together, fully explain the trauma of this break with the South's past. An examination of what took place in Louisiana may prove instructive.

The military occupation of part of Louisiana by Union forces began in the spring of 1862. President Abraham Lincoln was eager to install state governments in some of the occupied states as soon as possible, so he urged General Banks to register loyal voters and begin the Reconstruction process in Louisiana quickly. In an election held in February 1864, Michael Hahn, a Bavarian-born Unionist who had lived in New Orleans for many years, was elected governor, and legislators and six other state officials were also selected. James Madison Wells, a native of Rapides Parish, was chosen lieutenant governor and became governor a few months later when the legislature named Hahn to the United States Senate.

Banks next called for the election of delegates to a constitutional convention. Because of the Union defeat on Red River, the Convention of 1864 was dominated by delegates from New Orleans and the nearby parishes. The laboring classes of the city were well represented, so much so that the constitution adopted even included a minimum-wage provision, and the merchants of New Orleans were able to protect themselves, but the planters had a small voice as compared to the years before the war. The delegates to the Convention were as opposed to civil and political rights for blacks as any such gathering in Louisiana history; Unionism and belief in Negro suffrage did not go hand in hand. Under pressure from Banks they grudgingly ruled that the legislature might in the future expand the suffrage, but obviously there was little chance that suffrage would be given to blacks so long as the legislatures were elected by white Louisianians only.

When the Civil War ended, Unionists quickly lost control of Louisiana. In the elections held in 1865, the white men in those parts of the state that had been under Confederate control in 1864 could vote, as could those Louisianians who had been absent in Confederate service in 1864. Wells, who had moved over more and more to accommodate his views to the former Rebels, was re-elected governor, but the legislature had an overwhelming majority of men who had been strong Confederate sympathizers. Lincoln and Congress were far from agreement on how the former Confederate states should be handled, and Lincoln's death and the accession of Andrew Johnson to the presidency left policy more unsettled than ever. The so-called Radical Republicans in Congress were able to prevent the seating of senators and representatives from the southern states, but aside from that, each southern state was fully self-governing for two years. So accustomed did the people of Louisiana become to running their own affairs that, when a military Reconstruction policy was finally put in force in 1867, they regarded it as a repression. Two years earlier they would have taken it as a normal consequence of defeat.

Events in Washington played a major role in bringing on military Reconstruction, but the people of Louisiana unknowingly contributed to the growth of sentiment among the voters of the North demanding action to protect southern freedmen. The 1865 legislature proceeded to enact a version of the ''Black Codes'' that were being adopted by most of the former Confederate states. From the legislators' point of view, these codes gave legal status to former slaves, who had been in a legal limbo since emancipation. Included, however, was a vagrancy act that levied a fine for vagrancy and then provided that if the offender could not pay his fine, his labor could be sold to whoever did pay it. From the northern point of view that was an attempt to return the freedmen to slavery. From the southern point of view it was an attempt to get presumably idle blacks back to work, but the North had an army and navy, and its view would prevail.

In Louisiana, as in the rest of the South, the end of the Civil War brought a wave of violence directed at freedmen. Slaves had been fairly well protected from violence, except at the hands of their masters, because a slave's death or physical injury meant heavy financial loss. With emancipation and the war's end, however, that protection was gone. From 1865 until the middle of the twentieth century, there was, for all practical purposes, an open season on black males in Louisiana if the hunter was a white man. During the last half of 1865 and the first half of 1866, the murder of blacks was common, but ordinarily only one or two men were killed at a time. In July of 1866, however, a bloody riot broke out in New Orleans that focused northern public opinion, and therefore Congressional attention, upon the status of freedmen in the South.

The riot of July 30, 1866, resulted from an attempt to reconvene the Constitutional Convention of 1864. The constitution had a provision permitting the convention to be called back into session, probably for use in case voters had refused to ratify the document, but there was no time limit. By mid-1866 it had become obvious to the Unionists of Louisiana, native-born and immigrants from the North, that they would never again win office in the state without black suffrage. In addition, black leaders, mainly from the old free-Negro class, had been demanding suffrage since 1863. If the Convention of 1864 could be brought back into session, it might be willing to give the vote to blacks for the sake of the delegates' own political survival. Thus, Unionist leaders, by now synonymous with Radical Republican leaders in Louisiana, issued a call for the convention to reconvene at Mechanic's Institute on July 30, 1866.

The convention never actually went into session, because a quorum was not present at the time set in the call. During the delay, a parade of freedmen marched across Canal Street to the convention hall. A scuffle broke out, and the city police began firing into the mainly unarmed crowd. The freedmen took refuge in the hall, tried to hold the doors closed, and fought back with chair legs for a time. Eventually fire from the police, aided by firemen who identified themselves by white handkerchiefs tied about their arms, brought panic, and those who were able leaped through the windows and tried to run away. Many of them were shot down. In all, 3 white Unionists and 34 black ones had been killed, 17 whites and 119 blacks wounded. Former Governor Hahn was among the wounded, and two white Radical leaders, a minister named Horton and the fiery Dr. A. P. Dostie, were among the dead.

The New Orleans riot and other less spectacular instances of violence directed against Unionists finally convinced the people of the North that black men in the South needed protection. Such protection might have been provided by troops, but that would have meant maintaining an expensive army indefinitely. Republican leaders concluded that the best solution was to extend the right to vote to the black men of the South, so that they might defend themselves. Some Republican leaders, Thaddeus Stevens among them, realized that the vote was not enough and that blacks needed economic strength upon which to base political strength, but Congress was not prepared to go so far as to distribute land among the freedmen. In early 1867, however, Congress did proceed to pass the first of the Military Reconstruction Acts.

The South was divided into five military districts, each commanded by a major general. Louisiana and Texas made up the Fifth District, under General Philip Sheridan. Under the acts it was Sheridan's duty to register all adult males, black or white, who could swear that they had never voluntarily aided the Confederacy, and then hold an election for delegates to a constitutional convention. That led to the Constitutional Convention of 1867–1868 in Louisiana, made up of equal numbers of black and white delegates, which drew up the Constitution of 1868. That document was ratified in April of 1868. In the opinion of many students of Louisiana government, the Constitution of 1868 was the best that the state has ever had. It provided for representation in both houses of the legislature on the basis of total population, provided for the establishment of integrated public schools, and set up a well-organized court system.

State officials were elected at the same time that the new constitution was ratified, and Republicans were chosen. Before the end of the war, two free Negro brothers of New Orleans, Louis Charles and Joseph B. Roudanez, had begun publishing a bilingual Unionist newspaper, the *New Orleans Tribune,* which advocated Republicanism. As the war ended, Republican meetings became more and more frequent. Leaders of the party, originally, were native white Unionists, educated black men, and immigrants from the North, often called carpetbaggers. Gradually, the carpetbaggers, most of whom were young former officers of the Union army, won control of the new party. The Republican nominating convention of January 1868 nominated Henry Clay Warmoth for governor and Oscar J. Dunn, a Negro, for lieutenant governor. Warmoth won decisively, and the Republicans had a secure majority in the legislature.

Henry Clay Warmoth was only twenty-six years old when he became governor of Louisiana. He had had a distinguished record in the Union army and had risen to the rank of lieutenant colonel. After the Vicksburg campaign, General Grant accused him of exaggerating Union casualties and removed him from the army. Warmoth went to Washington, obtained an interview with President Lincoln, and recovered his rank. Sent to New Orleans to serve under Banks, he had functioned as provost judge. He and Grant cordially disliked each other for the remainder of their political lives, and the dislike was to have a definite effect upon the course of political Reconstruction in Louisiana. Warmoth was a young man of enormous charm; in Louisiana even his worst political enemies seem to have liked him personally. In fact, he shared many attitudes with white Louisianians, especially their firm belief in the inferiority of black people. His racism would in time contribute to his political demise, but he remained in Louisiana after Reconstruction, and in his eighties wrote his memoirs, in which he claimed that he had prevented the "Africanization" of his adopted state.

In November of 1868 it was time for a presidential election.

Democrats, North and South, hoped to defeat Grant, who became the Republican candidate, and thus end Radical Reconstruction before it had well begun. In Louisiana, since many Confederate sympathizers were disfranchised, the Democrats could hope for victory only if large numbers of black voters were persuaded to vote Democratic or were kept away from the polls altogether. An organization to accomplish this purpose, the Knights of the White Camellia, obviously modeled after the Ku Klux Klan, had been established in St. Mary Parish and had rapidly spread over the state. The KWC was so successful in intimidating black voters that Grant received only a handful of votes in a number of parishes where Warmoth had received a thousand or more. Horatio Seymour, the Democrat, carried Louisiana, but Grant was nonetheless elected president.

Obviously, no matter how many black Republicans there were in Louisiana, the Republicans could not maintain control of the state if the voters could be intimidated with impunity. Therefore, Warmoth promoted and the legislature passed a new election law, providing for a Returning Board to make the final tabulation of the vote. The board was given power to throw out the vote from any precinct or parish in which fraud or intimidation had taken place. Created to prevent the stealing of elections *by* the Democrats, in practice the Returning Board could be just as useful in stealing an election *from* the Democrats. Whether this was actually done, nobody knows. In every Louisiana election from 1868 through 1878 there was so much fraud, intimidation, and other skulduggery that it is impossible to say who won a majority of the votes actually cast or who would have won had an honest election been held. In passing, it might be noted that almost the same thing could be said for elections long after Reconstruction was over.

There is no evidence that Warmoth himself embezzled funds or accepted bribes, but other officials in his administration certainly did dip into the till. Warmoth was not a poor man when he became governor, but he was definitely a rich one when his term ended. He made his money through his majority ownership of the *New Orleans Republican,* which did official printing, and through buying and selling state securities. Through official actions Warmoth, as governor, could drive the price of state paper down or up. Therefore, when he dealt in warrants and treasury notes, he was not really speculating, but rather betting on an almost sure thing. In all fairness, however, it should be pointed out again that Louisiana governments before Warmoth had been corrupt and that Louisiana governments after Warmoth were corrupt. Furthermore, government in most other states of the Union, North as well as South, was corrupt during the Reconstruction period.

The earlier writers on Reconstruction emphasized the debts incurred by the Radical regimes and the taxes levied upon the people, treating these topics as if they were a manifestation of irresponsible tyranny in its worst form. Insofar as debts were concerned, a great deal of exaggeration occurred. Not counting the disallowed Confederate debt, Louisiana owed about $14 million at the end of the Civil War, most of it prewar in origin. During presidential Reconstruction, that figure rose to about $17.5 million. Warmoth's administration added about $7.5 million, bringing the total at the end of his term to about $25 million. It should not be thought that the state under Warmoth spent $7.5 million more than it took in. Actually, Louisiana's credit was so poor that bonds brought as little as fifty or sixty cents on the dollar when sold. It should be added that the state's debt was reduced somewhat under the Radical Republican Kellogg regime that followed Warmoth; it was then partially repudiated by the Democrats after they returned to power.

Taxes in Louisiana were much higher after the Civil War than they had been before, but taxes before the war had been abnormally low. The Radical regimes offered far more public services than their antebellum predecessors, and therefore government, even had there been no corruption at all, had to be much more expensive. Tax rates tell only half the story, however; the rate might be high, but taxes could still be low if assessments were low. Apparently, in New Orleans, by Louisiana standards, both rates and assessments were high; but in the rural parishes assessments were very low. It should be remembered also that depreciated state or city treasury notes could often be used for the payment of taxes, and since they could be bought at considerable discount, that was another factor in reducing the taxes actually paid. As high as they were, Louisiana tax rates were lower than those in most northern states, but the northern states came out of the Civil War more prosperous than they went in. Louisiana, on the other hand, was so impoverished that any tax was a burden.

Louisiana's Radical Republicans soon split into two factions. Warmoth, who built support with state patronage, was the obvious leader of one faction. The other faction was made up mainly of federal officeholders, most of them employed at the Custom House, but the postmaster was among them. They were generally referred to as the Custom House Ring. Probably a break was inevitable from the beginning, but two matters brought it into the open. James F. Casey, collector of customs, was Mrs. Ulysses S. Grant's brother-in-law, and he hoped to become United States senator from Louisiana. Warmoth threw his support to J. R. West, who was elected. More serious was the fact that Warmoth was totally unsympathetic to the civil-rights ambitions of the black people of Louisiana.

Oscar J. Dunn, the incorruptible black lieutenant governor, went over to the Custom House faction because of Warmoth's racial attitudes. That put Warmoth in real political danger, because, under the Constitution of 1868, the governor, if impeached, was suspended from office until after his trial. There was a distinct possibility that the Custom House Ring and the Democrats combined could muster enough votes in the House of Representatives to impeach. Dunn would then become governor until Warmoth had been tried by the Senate; the trial might be indefinitely delayed, and it was even possible that Dunn, with gubernatorial patronage at his disposal, might be able to achieve the two-thirds senatorial majority needed for conviction. Warmoth was saved by the sudden death of Dunn, which made it possible for Pinckney Benton Stewart Pinchback to become lieutenant governor. Pinchback, the son of a Mississippi planter by one of his slaves, was a political ally of Warmoth. Since the impeachment of Warmoth would put his ally in office as governor, and a black ally at that, the conservative Democrats were no longer willing to co-operate with the Custom House, and Warmoth continued in office.

The political maneuvering from 1870 to the election of 1872 was constant and almost Byzantine, but space is not available for its description. By 1872 it was obvious that Warmoth could not get the Republican nomination; that went to William Pitt Kellogg, a carpetbagger from Illinois who had been serving as United States senator from Louisiana. After much bargaining, the anti-Radical forces, including Warmoth, united behind the candidacy of a Democrat, John McEnery. Warmoth, still governor, was in full control of the electoral machinery, and almost every device imaginable, fair or foul, was used to reduce Kellogg's vote and to increase McEnery's, except that outright intimidation had to be used more subtly because the Fifteenth Amendment and federal legislation protected freedmen's right to vote. Probably, though not certainly, McEnery received a majority of the ballots that went into the boxes; probably, but again not certainly, in an honest election Kellogg would have had a majority.

The decision was up to the Returning Board, but shortly there were two returning boards, one dominated by Warmoth, which had custody of the official returns; the other dominated by the Radical Republicans. Lieutenant Governor Pinchback was unwilling to support Warmoth to the extent of putting a Democratic governor into office, and November 9, 1872, the House of Representatives voted Warmoth's impeachment, making Pinchback governor until the term ended in mid-January. Warmoth's returning board reported that McEnery had been elected, but the other board, without returns, declared Kellogg the victor. Already a United States District Court, presided over by a Radical Republican judge, had declared the Radical Returning Board the legal one, and, after the impeachment, the Grant administration recognized Pinchback as the legal governor of Louisiana. The Democrats, having stolen the election originally, were outraged that it was stolen back, but once Grant had recognized Pinchback's right to the gubernatorial office, the Democratic cause was lost. The Democrats maintained for more than two years that McEnery was the real governor of Louisiana, but for what the office was worth, Kellogg was assured of the governorship.

Kellogg's four years were almost a period of guerrilla warfare in Louisiana. At the beginning of his term, the opposition sought to bring him down by refusing to pay taxes, but that plan failed. A group of prominent New Orleanians, black and white, including former Confederate generals P. G. T. Beauregard and James Longstreet, sought accommodation by advocating equal division of public office between the two races, full protection of civil rights, and honest and economical government, but that Unification Movement was rejected by Democrats and Radicals alike. Violence was becoming more frequent throughout 1872 and early 1873, when a dispute over whether a Radical or a Democrat was entitled to be sheriff of Grant Parish led to the "Colfax Riot," in which at least sixty-nine blacks and perhaps as many as a hundred were killed, some twenty being executed after surrendering. The federal courts dismissed the conviction of some of the white participants on constitutional grounds. Since no Louisiana jury was going to convict a white man for killing a Negro, the decision meant that black men had no legal protection whatsoever against violence.

Neither, as it turned out, did white Republicans. In 1874, a new organization, the White League, came into being in Louisiana. The league was paramilitary, definitely not secret, and it maintained that the only real issue in Louisiana was whether whites or blacks should dominate state politics. Founded at Opelousas, the White League rapidly spread over the whole state. The Twitchells, a family from Vermont, had settled with relatives and friends in what became Red River Parish after the Civil War and, as Republicans, had come to dominate the parish politically. At Coushatta, the parish seat, a rumor spread in late August of 1874 that the blacks of the parish were planning to attack the white Democrats. The rumor was almost certainly unfounded, but it was believed, and a call for help was sent to neighboring parishes. Men came by the hundreds, some from as far away as Texas, most of them members of the White League. White Republican officeholders were put under protective custody and agreed to resign if given a guarantee of safe passage from the state. The guarantee was given, and five officeholders and one of their friends, under escort, set out for Texas on the morning of August 30. That afternoon, they were intercepted by a mob, an action obviously planned in advance by mob and escort, and the six Republicans were shot to shreds.

The culmination of organized violence came just two weeks after the Coushatta Massacre, with the Battle of Liberty Place in New Orleans. In the city the White League was organized into a regiment, and there existed another regiment of "militia" loyal to the McEnery government. The White League was buying arms from the North, and the Metropolitan Police, actually a militia loyal to the Kellogg government, sought to halt this influx of weapons. When a large shipment arrived on the steamboat *Mississippi,* General Longstreet, commander of the state forces, decided to make a stand. The Metropolitans and some black militia took up a position barring the way to the waterfront, and the White League and its allies accepted the challenge. As thousands of spectators from high windows and from boats on the river watched, a pitched battle, including artillery and Gatling guns, was fought. The White League was victorious, and although federal troops arrived the next day to restore order, it had been clearly demonstrated that a Radical Republican administration could not survive anywhere in Louisiana, not even in New Orleans, without the support of the United States Army.

Kellogg gave the state an honest administration, compared to Warmoth. He was himself personally honest, and no grandiose schemes for defrauding the state treasury were attempted. Venality continued in the legislature, but the governor made an effort to halt it there. He initiated an investigation of the state debt and rejected a number of claims as fraudulent, and he was able to reduce the debt and taxes significantly. Had it not been for the Panic of 1873 and the depression that followed, he might have been a much more effective reformer. The governor was blamed for all that went wrong, and his enemies gave him no credit for his positive accomplishments. He was, in fact, far more unpopular than Warmoth had ever been, probably because of his stand for civil rights.

For the gubernatorial campaign of 1876, the Republicans nominated former United States Marshal Stephen B. Packard, long the real leader of the Custom House Ring. The Democrats chose as their candidate "what was left of Francis T. Nicholls," a maimed Confederate hero and a prewar Whig. The Democrats laid their plans carefully. In parishes where they were certain to win, all that was necessary was to hold down the Republican vote—which meant the black vote—as much as possible. Other parishes they were certain to lose; there, the object was to get as many Democratic votes as possible, and they really made an effort to persuade blacks to vote Democratic. Finally, there were five parishes that normally could be expected to go Republican, though they might be turned around to the Democratic side by an all-out effort of persuasion, including intimidation as one of the chief means of persuasion. Even if the Returning Board should throw out the vote from these "bulldozed" parishes, the Democrats would have lost nothing.

The Democratic plan was successful in that a majority of the votes reported were for Nicholls, but of course the Republicans challenged the result. The Louisiana election came to have national importance, because the disputed electoral vote from three southern states, including Louisiana, would decide whether Democrat Samuel J. Tilden or Republican Rutherford B. Hayes would become president of the United States. This is not the place for a discussion of the Compromise of 1877 that put Hayes into the White House, except as it applied to Louisiana. Louisiana's electoral vote, like the other disputed ones, was counted for Hayes, but Hayes withdrew all federal troops. When the troops left, Packard's hopes went with them. The chairman of the Republican national committee telegraphed Packard, urging him to create an incident that would require federal intervention, even if he had to die in the street. Packard wired back: "Your very polite invitation . . . 'to die in the street' is received. Owing to other pressing engagements I am constrained to decline, but would suggest the propriety of your coming to officiate in person." [1] Ironically, although Nicholls was recognized as governor, Kellogg, who had been elected by the Packard legislature, was again seated in Washington as United States senator from Louisiana.

Politically, Reconstruction was over in Louisiana, and it was an almost absolute failure. Impetus had been given to public schools, but it would be more than a generation later before further improvement would take place, except for a few of the larger towns. For a quarter century after 1877 education for blacks was not so good as in the Kellogg era. The state had a better constitution than before the war, but the process of rewriting it began in 1879, and by 1970 the Louisiana constitution had become a monstrosity of more than a thousand pages of fine print, full of contradictions, and so inelastic that as many as fifty amendments a year were being offered to the voters. Politically, the black man had received the vote, and it had been guaranteed to him by the Fifteenth Amendment. In practice, however, in Louisiana his vote was neutralized by fraud and intimidation from 1876 through 1896, and then, in 1898, a new set of voting qualifications disfranchised all but a very few blacks. Corruption of the political process, though certainly not unfamiliar to Louisianians before the Civil War, was practiced so consistently by both sides during Reconstruction that it became habit, a constant feature of Louisiana politics for altogether too many years.

Perhaps the worst effect of Reconstruction was the legacy of hatred that it left behind. The horrors of Radical Republican rule became the stock in trade of Democratic politicians for more than a generation. Constant reiteration made the memory more and more horrible in the minds of people who had not been born when Radical rule ended. Eventually, even the North was converted to the southern version of that period of American history, and relations between the races were poisoned in the North as well as in the South. The miasma of suspicion and distrust left behind has not yet dissipated.

1. *New Orleans Daily Picayune,* January 16, 1877.

8

Living with Despair:
Social and Economic Developments
after the Civil War

*T*HE effects of the Civil War have been felt in Louisiana ever since the struggle ended, but obviously they were felt more keenly by the generation that lived from the end of the war to the turn of the century. It was possible to prosper economically in postwar Louisiana, but it was difficult. All people and classes, including those of New Orleans, felt economic hardship and a degree of stultification. Black people were no longer slaves, but most of them became laborers on sugar plantations or sharecroppers on cotton plantations, and the material conditions of their lives were probably worse than they had been on a well-run and prosperous plantation in 1860. Of all classes, however, the yeoman farmer lost most. He felt the damage of the war as much as any other white, and added to this was a growing alienation from the national economy, because, as agriculture became more commercialized, the subsistence farmer became more and more an anachronism. Many lost their land and became sharecroppers, and eventually the farmer, as opposed to the planter, would disappear from the scene, but that would not be until the twentieth century.

The post-Civil War period saw important social and cultural

developments. Public education was in the doldrums from the end of Reconstruction until the turn of the century, and advances in the private and parochial area of education were slight. Racial segregation, begun before the war, seems to have increased geometrically after Reconstruction, and by 1900 had reached the state of degradation and discrimination at which it would remain until the Second Reconstruction of the 1960s. The situation was part of an increasingly bitter racism, abetted in part by northern public opinion, which manifested itself in frequent lynchings and in at least two instances of massacres of blacks—events comparable to some of the worst moments of Reconstruction.

Economically, sugar plantations, which had been harder hit by the war than cotton plantations, gradually recovered, only to be dashed into despair when President Grover Cleveland saw to it that the federal bounty on Louisiana sugar was repealed. Cotton recovered from natural disasters immediately after the war only to face a gradual but inexorable decline in prices continuing into the 1890s. Sharecropping and the crop-lien system developed as a necessary labor-and-credit system, but took on life of their own and persisted down to World War II. A new staple appeared on the scene in the 1880s when the prairies of southwest Louisiana became a great rice-producing area. At the same time, however, timber companies, mostly northern, were denuding the swamps of cypress and the hills of pine and hardwoods, leaving behind almost a desert in some of the hill areas.

Some economic progress took place. River traffic was quickly restored after the end of hostilities; railroads were restored, and before 1900 the rails had reached practically every part of the state able to support traffic, in the process opening up new lands to agriculture. Roads remained execrable until the second quarter of the twentieth century. New Orleans continued to be the main outlet for American cotton and grain going abroad, but it would hardly be correct to say that the city prospered. Sickly, misgoverned, swamped in debt, New Orleans continued to exist. Entertainment, moral and immoral, continued to be abundantly available, and the people of the Crescent City were capable of great gaiety at carnival time, but there, as in the rest of the state, the over-all quality of life was low. Louisianians, except for a fortunate few, existed and endured as best they could, but they did not dream great dreams or strive for great things. The Acadians and the other plain folk of South Louisiana retained the capacity to enjoy themselves, but they too suffered economic privation and social and cultural isolation.

Blacks, as the war ended, tended to drift back to the plantation, though not necessarily the one from which they had come. Moving from one plantation to another was one way of demonstrating their freedom, though the sharecrop system would curtail even that freedom in a short time. Louisianians were convinced that many freedmen did not work, but that belief seems to have resulted from a shortage of labor rather than from laborers withholding themselves from the market. A migration of blacks from the poorer lands of the southeastern states began immediately after the war and continued for many years. In the number of blacks brought into Louisiana, the migration apparently matched or exceeded prewar migration and the slave trade.

Yeoman farmers left few records, and they did not attract the attention of observers, domestic and foreign, to the same degree as freedmen. Our somewhat sketchy knowledge of them in the years following the Civil War is derived largely from census records and from tax-assessment rolls. In one way or another, the war disturbed the lives of nearly every family; a farm suffered if its owner was hiding out in the woods, though not so much as if he was in uniform hundreds of miles away. Certainly many families were on short rations the first year after the war, and some of them for longer than that, but in time the farmer once again grew enough corn for his family's needs, acquired a mule or some oxen for plowing his land, and was back at a Spartan subsistence level. The yeomen soon became just as entrapped in the crop-lien system as other agriculturists, however, and with the passage of time, many of them lost their land and became sharecroppers; since they were prolific, the sons of those who held their land often were forced into tenantry.

Because the census of 1870 listed sharecroppers as independent farmers, it was long believed that the Civil War resulted in breaking up many of the great plantations into smaller farms. Such was not the case; on the contrary, the consolidation of landholdings that had begun long before the war continued afterward and even continues in the 1970s. The plantation definitely survived, but it did not necessarily remain in the hands of the antebellum owner. Sugar plantations in particular tended to change hands, because the capital required to restore them to production was often beyond the means of the former owners. A family was more likely to be able to hold a cotton plantation, because the capital needed to accumulate the necessary tools and work animals for cotton was not so great. Also, the demand for cotton at war's end was such that credit was easily available. Even so, most of the old planter families gradually sold out or lost out as new men began to control cotton planting. The profits from supplying tenants and from ginning and buying cotton became at least as important as any profits realized from cultivating the crop—probably more important. Also, plantation agriculture began to move westward out of the alluvial regions of North Louisiana as the hardwood hill country was planted in cotton. Plantations in the hills came into being through the consolidation of smaller farms into large units. Under cultivation these lands were easily exhausted and highly subject to erosion. By the mid-twentieth century row cultivation had been largely abandoned in the hills, and the fields had been converted to pasture. The new hill planters of the nineteenth century might be immigrants from the East or merchants who had acquired land from their debtors. A few were local men with the right combination of skill, energy, luck, and acquisitive instinct.

Its resistance to Radical Reconstruction having given it prestige, the commercial class of New Orleans gained economic power with the increasing commercialization of agriculture. The Crescent City was especially hard hit by the Panic of 1873 and the depression that followed, but recovery finally came. Most of the city's banks were strong enough to ride out the storm. New Orleans had few families of really great wealth, however, and the upper crust of society did not engage in the gaucheries of the *nouveaux riches* of the cities of the Northeast. Good restaurants continued to abound, but except for eating out and attending the theater and the opera, most people found entertainment at home. Mardi Gras continued to be a local carnival time of fun until late in the nineteenth century, when increased wealth and an awareness of the occasion as a tourist attraction led to its greater elaboration. Social position and wealth came to determine the carnival krewe to which one belonged and the balls that one attended.

Obviously, most citizens of New Orleans were not of the upper class. Middle-class citizens continued, as before the war, to strive for upper-class status, sometimes succeeding, more often failing. Labor in the city was more militant than one might expect. In the 1880s the Knights of Labor came into New Orleans and enjoyed considerable success there and in the sugar fields until the failure of a strike in 1886. Within the city a general strike was largely successful in 1892, with white and black workers co-operating. Two years later, however, when British cotton-shippers attempted to replace white wharf workers with lower-paid blacks, riots between white and black workers broke out and continued sporadically through the spring of 1895. The number of deaths in these clashes is unknown, but nine blacks were known to have been killed, and there was no counting of the number of bodies on the bottom of the river. Racism had proved much stronger than class interest.

Smaller towns came somewhere between New Orleans on the one hand and the countryside on the other; but, in general, they were more closely akin to the countryside than to the city. Baton Rouge, which became the state capital again in 1879, grew rapidly, as did Shreveport. They and smaller towns prospered because, as the general merchants became more important, the planters tended more and more to do business close to home rather than dealing directly with New Orleans. In fact, a significant difference between the antebellum small town and the postbellum one was the greater importance of the merchant class.

Membership in white churches grew steadily, but the most important religious development in Louisiana during Reconstruction and after was the withdrawal of black members from the existing churches to form churches of their own. The Catholic church beyond New Orleans and some of the South Louisiana towns and Episcopal and Presbyterian churches everywhere lost almost all their black members. Most blacks became Baptists, but Methodism also flourished among them. The resulting voluntary segregation of black Christianity was significant for two reasons: in the first place, it separated black and white in one of the most important areas of life, thus making mutual understanding ever more difficult; second, and on the positive side, it provided an area in which blacks could be completely free from white domination. It is no accident that black leadership in Louisiana and the nation in the last century has tended to come from the churches, because there leaders had an opportunity to develop.

The Constitution of 1868 had set up a public school system and required that the public schools admit pupils regardless of race, but except for those in New Orleans, public schools were of low quality, often taught by poorly qualified teachers, and they remained open only a few months of the year. As bad as public education was during Reconstruction, it became much worse afterward. The Bourbons who ruled Louisiana until after the turn of the century would probably have liked to do away with public schools altogether, but they did not dare go so far. They did insist, however, that Louisiana was too poor to have good schools and that taxes must be kept low to attract industry. They did keep taxes low, but they did not attract industry, and they did not provide good schools. Louisiana was the only state in the United States in which white illiteracy increased between 1880 and 1890, and the only one in which black illiteracy remained above 70 percent in 1890. Private and parochial schools took up part of the slack in education, but not enough. Even in the 1970s, there is evidence of what Louisiana has suffered in neglecting education from the end of Reconstruction into the second decade of the twentieth century.

Another characteristic of the years following the Civil War was the growth of racism in Louisiana. The state's society had been racist from the time the first African slave arrived because one of the basic justifications of slavery was belief that the

Negro was an inferior human being. But, despite many exceptions, slavery had a definitely paternalistic side; relationships between master and slave frequently were truly affectionate. Those who did not own slaves were characterized by Negrophobia to some degree, and there was much friction between black and white workers, mainly white Irishmen, in New Orleans before the Civil War. Negrophobia, supposedly confined to less prosperous whites before the war, afterward permeated all levels of white society. Some elements of paternalism remained, but eventually it became socially impossible to speak out in favor even of simple justice for blacks. George Washington Cable tried to do so, and he was forced out of the state he loved.

One manifestation of the increasing bitterness of race relations was increasing segregation. There had been beginnings of segregation, especially in the churches, before the Civil War. In New Orleans, blacks, slave or free, were required to ride certain designated streetcars, marked by a star, until General Sheridan put an end to the practice. The segregation of churches after 1865 was by choice of black Christians. In New Orleans, the schools were completely segregated after the Radical Republicans were driven from power. In the years that followed, segregation was imposed by custom in more and more areas of life, and the customs were more often than not enacted into law. Railroad trains and riverboats were two special areas of conflict, but the problem of the steamboats became less pressing after 1880 as the role of these craft in transportation was reduced. In time the legislature required that railroad coaches be segregated, and it was the defiance of that law by a Louisiana Negro that led the United States Supreme Court to rule, in *Plessy* v. *Ferguson,* that separate but equal accommodations for the two races did not violate the Fourteenth Amendment. By the beginning of the twentieth century, patterns of segregation were as rigid in Louisiana as in other southern states.

Louisiana Negroes were politically powerless after 1876; they were completely disfranchised in 1898. The practice of segregation reminded them daily of their inferiority in the eyes of whites. Apparently, any possible threat to white supremacy had been removed. Yet the practice of lynching grew with the passage of the years. Lynching had certainly not been unknown in antebellum Louisiana, but before the Civil War, whites and blacks were launched into eternity with impartiality; after the war, most victims, though not all, were black. There is a myth that Negroes were lynched for raping or attempting to rape white women, but there were more lynchings for murder than for rape, and some black men died horrible deaths for simple theft. Not all, in fact, were men; a woman accused of attempting to poison a white family was burned at the stake. How many lynchings there were cannot be said. The official count is high enough, but many were never reported.

The most famous Louisiana lynching, however, was of Italians, not of Negroes. In October of 1890, Police Chief Dave Hennessy of New Orleans was murdered in gangland fashion after he had begun an investigation of the Mafia in his city. Nine men were arrested and charged with the murder, all of them Italians. The evidence against seven of them, if the newspapers of the time can be believed, was almost conclusive, but the jury at the trial in March 1891, acquitted six of the nine and were unable to reach a decision on the other three. The people of New Orleans were outraged at what they considered a miscarriage of justice; undoubtedly, prejudice against Italians played a role in their reaction. The morning after the verdict a notice appeared in the newspapers inviting the public to attend a vigilante meeting, and hundreds responded. The mob, for such the men attending the meeting quickly became, rushed to the parish prison, broke down the wooden rear door, and seized eleven prisoners, five of whom had not yet been tried. Two were hanged and the remainder shot to death. The Italian government lodged a formal protest, but apparently the people of New Orleans believed that justice had been done. One newspaper, discussing the protest, pointed out that "residence in the Pelican State entailed for anybody a certain amount of danger, and the 'foreigners who come to this country must take the same risk with natives.' " [1]

Though Louisiana never recovered economically from the

---

1. Quoted in William Ivy Hair, *Bourbonism and Agrarian Protest: Louisiana Politics, 1877–1900* (Baton Rouge: Louisiana State University Press, 1969).

Civil War, there was advancement over the depths of 1865. New Orleans had begun to revive in 1863, with the opening of the Mississippi River, and the end of the war brought even more trade, with the opening of the Red River and the Arkansas. Of importance, too, was the deepening of the channel into the Gulf from the Mississippi by Captain James B. Eads's jetties. Before the jetties were built, it was not unusual for ocean-going ships to have to wait weeks, or even months, to get into or out of the mouth of the river because of mud deposited in times of high water. The jetties narrowed the river, thus increasing the velocity of the current, and scouring out a deeper channel. Better railroad connections, particularly the Southern Pacific, aided commerce. On the other hand, New Orleans did not grow as rapidly as cities with which it might have been comparable in 1860. Partly that was because of epidemics, partly because of misgovernment, but mainly the city's slow growth was caused by the fact that it remained commercial when cities in the North were becoming more and more industrialized.

There were many attempts at railroad building during Reconstruction, and the main prewar lines were put back into good running order. The only new line within the state, however, was the Mobile and Chattanooga—later called the Louisiana and Texas—which came from Mobile to New Orleans, then ran up the west bank of the Mississippi to Bayou Goula, just above Donaldsonville. After Reconstruction was over, the old Opelousas Line was pushed on westward along the Teche and across the prairies to Texas. It eventually became part of the Southern Pacific. At almost the same time, the prewar Vicksburg, Shreveport, and Texas made its way across North Louisiana from Monroe to Shreveport. Further access to the west was provided by a union between the Louisiana and Texas and the old Baton Rouge, Grosse Tete, and Opelousas. A line up the east bank of the Mississippi provided transportation for the abundant cotton crops of the Mississippi Delta north of Vicksburg, making railroads as important as the river in bringing goods to New Orleans. The steamboat gradually disappeared, but it was replaced by tugboats and barges carrying far more tonnage than the more romantic stern-wheelers.

Originally, almost all of Louisiana had been abundantly

blessed with forests, and the cutting of cypress out of the swamps of South Louisiana and pine from the hills and flats of the Florida Parishes had become fairly important before the Civil War. After the war the harvesting of cypress was renewed, and Shreveport, Plaquemine, and New Orleans all became important cypress-milling centers. The Atchafalaya Swamp was the main source of cypress logs, and apparently it was every man for himself in cutting the huge trees. They had taken centuries to grow, and they made lumber that was practically impervious to decay. Rafts of logs of enormous size floated on the rivers and bayous. One came to New Orleans made up of a hundred and fifty logs, each of them at least fifty feet long, and containing, altogether, more than a million board feet. The supply must have seemed inexhaustible, but it was not; soon after the turn of the century, the cypress forests were gone. A few trees are beginning to reach a minimum size for cutting now, nearly a century later, but it is doubtful that the day of an almost everlasting cypress board fence or roof of cypress shingles can ever return.

Worst of all was the destruction of Louisiana's pine forests, which had covered the highlands and flats of much of the Florida Parishes and Southwest Louisiana, as well as the hills west of the Mississippi and north of the Red. The great timber companies that cut out the white pine forests of the Great Lakes region moved into Louisiana to continue their work with yellow pine. Bogalusa and Lake Charles became large lumber towns, but literally hundreds of other sawmill communities sprang into being, flourished for a while, and then disappeared. Others have managed to survive, but only as a shadow of their former selves, deserted by younger people and inhabited by older men and women who have nowhere else to go. Where the hardwoods were cut, crops could usually be planted, and other trees of less value grew up where the cypress had been, but the pine lands were too poor for farming. Thus the lumber companies left behind them a desert. Some areas are still desert; but since the 1950s, the use of pine for paper pulp has resulted in the rehabilitation of much of the cut-over area.

Louisiana continued to be primarily agricultural. The restoration of sugar production required more capital than the restoration of cotton plantations; that and the fact that a significant proportion of a crop had to be saved for use as seed cane made recovery slow. Planters were also plagued by a shortage of labor; much black labor was brought in from the southeastern states and some workers came from abroad, but the demand kept wages high. General Banks and the the Freedmen's Bureau had attempted to establish a wage system on sugar plantations, and in the long run that was successful. Planters and laborers would probably have preferred some sort of sharecropping system, but the industrial nature of sugar production required a highly disciplined labor force working in large gangs. Sugar plantation workers continued to live in the former slave quarter and to work in gangs much as they had before the war. Wages were fairly good for the time, fifteen dollars to eighteen dollars per month for prime men with rations furnished, twenty-five to thirty dollars if the worker fed himself. Women, older men, and children received wages in proportion. The planter always provided a house and usually a store that advanced goods to his hands on credit, normally at very high prices.

Wages in the sugar fields remained fairly stable, despite efforts by planters to reduce them. The shortage of labor was such that one plantation was almost certain to break an agreement to pay no more than a certain amount. During the early 1880s there were several strikes protesting attempted cuts or for higher pay scales in the parishes along the Mississippi, but they were not successful. In the middle of the decade the Knights of Labor, which had become established in New Orleans, began to organize the cane-field workers, black and white. When the planters refused to negotiate with the union, a strike was called at the beginning of the harvest period of 1886, a year that brought a bumper crop to the cane fields.

The planters refused to consider negotiations, and the strike continued well into November. The workers did not give in when evicted from their cabins, but gathered in the sugar-country towns, especially Thibodaux. On November 21 a light freeze put a film of ice on standing puddles of water and a chill of fear into the hearts of the planters, who saw the possibility of a hard freeze destroying the best crop since the Civil War.

Judge Taylor Beattie, who had earlier run for governor on the

Republican ticket and advocated black political rights, had organized vigilante committees and had imported armed men, reportedly experienced "nigger killers" from Shreveport, to break the strike. Shooting of Negroes began on the night of November 22 and continued through the morning of the next day. At the end it was reported that thirty blacks had been killed and more than a hundred wounded. In reality, the account of the number dead and wounded was almost certainly too low; a New Orleans reporter told of seeing many other bodies. The strike was broken, and the crop was harvested.

The late nineteenth and early twentieth century saw definite changes in the organization of the sugar industry. Corporations took over more and more plantations, and the sugar mills became larger and more efficient. Since the small planter's sugar house could not compete with the corporations' mills, more and more plantations gave up sugar-making and sold the cane they grew by the ton. In time planters began to form co-operatives to handle their cane, and practically all the "grinding" was done in mills operated by co-operatives or by corporations. In time field operations became highly mechanized, although that did not take place until well into the twentieth century. As the nineteenth century drew to an end, sugar-growing was still the work primarily of black field hands and mules.

Cotton cultivation after the Civil War followed a different course from that of sugar cane. At war's end, the price of cotton was very high, and most planters were able to borrow the money they needed to put in a crop and to pay wages to field hands as the Freedmen's Bureau preferred. In 1866 a flood destroyed much cotton and kept a great deal of land under water until it was too late to plant a second crop. In areas where a second crop was planted, or where the first crop escaped the flood, army worms destroyed the plants before they had had time to mature. The sequence of events in 1867 was almost exactly the same as in 1866, exhausting the capital and credit of cotton planters and many yeoman farmers.

Under these conditions, planters could not possibly pay wages to the freedmen who did the work on the cotton plantations; and after 1866 the workers, many of whom had gone unpaid, were largely opposed to a wage system. Sharecropping became the system of labor in the cotton fields. It is difficult to see how, without the development of sharecropping, the cultivation of cotton could have been revived in Louisiana after the Civil War. It is significant that it was desired by the freedmen as well as the planters; indeed, many planters were opposed in principle and engaged in sharecropping only through necessity. Probably it was a necessary transition from slave labor to free labor. However, sharecropping became an entrenched system, leaving many southern blacks and eventually more southern whites in a kind of peonage well into the twentieth century.

The system was deceptively simple. The planter provided land, a cabin on the land the sharecropper worked (thus breaking up the slave quarter on cotton plantations), work stock, tools, and seed. The sharecropper provided his labor and that of his family and was expected to provide his own and his family's food and clothes. Without cash for food, clothing, and such small luxuries as were available, he bought these items from the plantation store, usually called a commissary, or from a general merchant designated by the planter. At the end of the year the planter and the sharecropper divided the cropper's crop on a half-and-half basis. The tenant never realized his half in cash, because he had to pay for the supplies he had bought during the year, and it was not unusual for him to end the year in debt. The laws of the state were quickly adjusted to protect the planter or merchant to whom the sharecropper owed money; so long as the tenant was in debt, he could not move without the creditor's permission, thus being reduced to more or less the status of a serf.

Inextricably entwined with the sharecropping system was the crop lien. The value of farm land in Louisiana was so reduced at the end of the Civil War that land was not satisfactory security for the credit that the cotton producer, whether planter or yeoman farmer, needed. Therefore the creditor took a lien—a mortgage, if one prefers that term—on the producer's crop. Yeoman farmers usually dealt with a nearby general merchant, and as noted, many planters arranged with general merchants for their sharecroppers to be provided with such goods as they needed. The planter, if he operated a commissary, bought from a wholesaler on credit or, in a few instances, borrowed directly from a bank. In every case the creditor's security was the crop that was being grown.

Under this system the granting of credit would normally begin before the crop for the year was planted, so the creditor's security was cotton that existed only in the plans of the debtor. Sickness, flood, insects, or even an unusually cold or wet spring could destroy or greatly reduce this crop. Furthermore, its value was subject to the fluctuations of a world market over which neither planter nor merchant had any control whatsoever. Under these conditions, interest rates on credit advanced had to be high—and they were high. It was said that such interest ran from 25 percent to grand larceny, which was not far from the truth. Rates of such magnitude added greatly to the costs of planters, farmers, and sharecroppers and prevented their accumulating capital. Thus the crop lien was self-perpetuating, and it exists to this day, though mechanization and greater prosperity have brought interest rates down to reasonable levels.

No labor actions like those in the cane country of the 1880s appeared in the cotton fields. The blacks of the cotton country had largely exhausted their capacity for protest in the "Kansas Fever" of 1879. "Kansas Fever" was a mass movement of blacks, mainly from Louisiana and Mississippi, to Kansas. It reached such proportions that planters who had once asserted a need to rid Louisiana of Negroes patrolled the roads to turn back would-be emigrants. In the long run, nearly all of those who went to Kansas came back south. The climate was not to their taste, and they did not have the skills needed in the wheat fields. No preparations had been made for receiving them. Most important of all, however, those who emigrated discovered that the people of Kansas, however sympathetic they might be to the plight of Negroes in Louisiana, showed conventional prejudice against those who came to Kansas.

The planter survived under the sharecrop and crop-lien system, and the concentration of landholdings continued. It has been suggested that planters made money, not from the production of cotton, but from the profits they made by selling to their tenants. Certainly the general merchants away from New Orleans, who had been of lesser importance in the economy of antebellum Louisiana, became a very important part of the state's economy after the war. Being a general merchant was risky, and probably more would-be merchants went bankrupt than prospered, but those who prospered tended to do extremely well. More often than not they operated a commercial cotton gin and bought and sold cotton as well as keeping store. When a church and a school were built nearby, a community came into being, often bearing the name of the merchant. Most general merchants in time acquired land, usually small farms that they took over from bankrupt yeoman farmers. Eventually they owned as many acres as the planters, and it might be difficult to tell which was which, except that frequently the merchant family's landholdings were not contiguous.

The postwar period saw a new system for marketing cotton come into being. The New Orleans factors declined in importance rather rapidly. Many were bankrupted by the loss of advances made on the disastrous crops of 1866 and 1867, but the trans-Atlantic cable and the completion of the telegraph network across the South really destroyed the factor. A cotton buyer in the interior could know the price of cotton in Liverpool just as quickly as a factor in New Orleans. He might even be able to pay a higher price for the cotton, because he did not depend on the profits from buying and selling alone, usually having a general store, a gin, and his own lands as additional sources of profit. With the establishment of the cotton exchange, the surviving factors tended to become brokers; their previous function as representatives of the planters had come to an end.

The 1880s saw the establishment of a new staple crop in Louisiana, or perhaps it would be better to say in a new part of Louisiana, since some rice had been grown for sale in Plaquemines Parish, along Bayou Lafourche, and in ponds in the Breaux Bridge district for many years. Parenthetically, it should be added that the Breaux Bridge rice ponds still serve a useful purpose; the crop produced in them now is crayfish, a delicacy much enjoyed by Louisianians. The new rice-growing region was the prairies of Southwest Louisiana, which for years had been thought useful only for cattle grazing.

After the Civil War a number of land companies bought lands in western Louisiana, the most important being the North American Land and Timber Company, actually a British corporation. That company and several others formed a syndicate that hired Seaman A. Knapp, president of Iowa Agricultural College, to determine whether the prairies in Southwest Louisiana could not be made useful agriculturally. Knapp discovered that an almost impervious layer of clay lay beneath the topsoil of the prairies and realized that this would simplify the flooding of rice fields. He quickly discovered that rice would thrive in Southwest Louisiana. The companies, desiring to sell their lands at good prices, sponsored excursions from New Orleans on the newly completed Southern Pacific Railroad, and a large number of middle-westerners took advantage of the opportunity to look over the prairies. Many of them decided to become rice farmers, leading to rapid settlement of Southwest Louisiana by immigrants of extremely high quality. Middle-westerners were better able to go into rice farming because they had more capital than Louisianians and because they were accustomed to grain machinery. Southwest Louisiana quickly became one of the major rice-producing areas of the United States. Thus, before the beginning of the twentieth century, Louisiana had a third staple crop to go with the traditional cotton and sugar.

The development of rice cultivation was one of the few optimistic notes in Louisiana during the last third of the nineteenth century. Cotton prices declined almost constantly, and cotton farmers and many planters became desperate. The lot of the sharecropper, black or white, grew worse with the passage of the years. Sugar planters did very well into the 1890s, though their labor was sullen and discontented after 1886; but then, in the 1890s, Congress did away with the federal bounty on sugar grown in the United States, and many planters faced bankruptcy. Some improvements came to New Orleans, but crime, corruption, and disease continued to outweigh progress. The fortunes of the smaller towns went up or down, mostly down, with the fortunes of agriculture.

If people had had a choice, the latter part of the nineteenth century was not the time in history most Louisianians would have chosen to live. Despair had the upper hand over hope, and men's minds were twisted by poverty and fear. Louisiana had always been a violent place, but the violence of the late nineteenth century had a sort of madness about it, a streak of senselessness when compared to the defense of "honor" in antebellum times and the political terrorism of Reconstruction. Dissent was no more permitted than before the Civil War, and George Washington Cable and the few lesser dissenters had to leave the state. Literature languished; the best writing was the political polemics of newspapers. Religion emphasized form over content, or resorted to revivalistic patterns that almost completely ignored the conditions in which men and women lived. Discontent manifested itself politically before the century was over, but the attempt at reform failed; another third of a century would pass before reform would come in pattern-breaking form.

9

Bourbonism, Agrarianism, and Racism: Louisiana Politics, 1877 to 1900

AS the years from the end of the Civil War to the turn of the century brought constant economic hardship and spreading social and cultural stagnation to the common people of Louisiana, political developments from the end of Reconstruction to 1900 provided no compensation. The reaction to Radical Republican corruption did not bring honest government; rather, it brought other beneficiaries to the practice of corruption. The alliance of great planters, New Orleans politicians, and the corrupting special interests of the convict-lease system and the Louisiana Lottery formed in the 1860s remained in power through electoral fraud more blatant and more effective than anything practiced by the Radical Republicans at their gamiest. Black votes in much of the state became nothing more than units to be added to the Democratic total at election time.

Francis T. Nicholls was undisputed governor of Louisiana from April of 1877 until Louis Wiltz took office in 1880. Nicholls was an aristocrat, unswervingly conservative in his political and fiscal ideas, a believer in *noblesse oblige* in dealing with the black people of the state, but nonetheless an unquestioning believer in white supremacy. He had promised during his campaign to respect the civil rights of Louisiana's blacks; and insofar as it lay in his power, he did seek to preserve those rights as he understood them. As a result of his beliefs concerning the treatment of Negroes—relatively liberal beliefs in the climate of opinion existing in Louisiana in the late 1870s—Nicholls earned the hatred and contempt of many members of his own party. On one occasion, he was even stoned by a mob in Baton Rouge.

It must not be thought that black participation in politics ended abruptly with the end of Radical Republican rule. The right of blacks to vote was recognized, at least verbally, by the now dominant Democrats. A few parishes with large Negro populations continued to elect Republican officials for a number of years, and black legislators participated in law-making well into the 1890s. The existence of these Negro officeholders probably served the interests of the Democratic leaders; the constant theme of white politicians was the danger of a return to Radical rule, and the presence of a few black officeholders seemed to support this cry of danger.

The term *Bourbon* is used to describe the politicians of Louisiana and the South as a whole from the end of Reconstruction to about the turn of the century. The term originates, of course, from the name of the French royal family which "never learned anything and never forgot anything." In other states the Bourbons combined political reaction in domestic politics with a "New South" appeal to northern capital and encouragement of industrialization. In Louisiana little more than lip service was given to the New South concept. Louisiana politicos were almost wholly reactionaries, constantly preaching hatred of the North, love of the Confederacy, and the danger of black rule.

An extremely important part of the Bourbon political machine was the Louisiana Lottery, a company chartered as a monopoly by the Radical Republican legislature of 1868. Its leaders saw before 1876 that the days of Radical Republicanism were numbered, however, and in the election of 1876 they contributed to Nicholls's campaign. More important, the lottery provided funds that kept Nicholls's administration in existence during the period of dual government when no revenues could be collected. The Louisiana Lottery could well afford gifts to Nicholls's government. It took in from hopeful souls all over the United States between twenty and thirty million dollars a year and paid out less than 50 percent of the take in prizes. It paid no taxes, and it paid the state only forty thousand dollars a year for the right to operate. It was by far the most available source of ready funds for aspiring politicians, and Major E. A. Burke was the agent through whom political deals were made.

For a decade Burke was the political boss of Louisiana. His origins are obscure; he apparently awarded himself his rank, and he may even have been from Illinois. He almost certainly was not the former Confederate officer he claimed to be. He was state treasurer, elected with Nicholls, and he published the *New Orleans Times.* When the *New Orleans Democrat,* chief journalistic opponent of the lottery, had financial trouble, Burke bought it, with lottery help, and made the new *Times-Democrat* the voice of Bourbonism and the lottery in Louisiana.

Despite the role the lottery had played in redemption, Governor Nicholls was opposed to it; and in 1879, he signed a bill passed by the legislature, abolishing the company's charter. Charles T. Howard, New Orleans agent for the New York lottery syndicate of Charles H. Murray and Company, parent company of the Louisiana Lottery, immediately went to the federal courts, however, and obtained a temporary restraining order. There followed an almost incredible demonstration of lottery power. A constitutional convention met, gave the lottery a twenty-five-year charter, and shortened the terms of all state officials except Burke by one year. Burke's term was extended until 1884.

Delegates to the 1879 convention would have liked to abolish universal manhood suffrage, but they did not yet dare. Republicans continued to elect some local officials and a few legislators in some areas. That was compensated for, however, by many restrictions put upon the legislature and upon local officials, and by extensive powers given to the governor. Governors under the Constitution of 1879 had powers as great as those Henry Clay Warmoth had amassed, including the right to succeed themselves, but those who held the office were weak men who did not make full use of their powers. Since the governors were dominated by the lottery and other special interests, however, local officials could not do any great harm to these interests. Finally, New Orleans in 1879 ceased to be the state capital, and Baton Rouge once more became the seat of government.

Already the legislature had adopted new election laws. The Returning Board was abolished, but the system that replaced it was at least as subject to fraud as its predecessor and as much under gubernatorial control. Significantly, the law provided no penalty for falsifying election returns. The purpose of such legislation, if not already apparent, certainly became clear after the election of 1878. Natchitoches Parish, which had normally cast a large Republican vote, reported not a single one. In fact, the most substantial Democratic vote came from those alluvial North Louisiana parishes that had been the source of the largest number of Republican votes during the Radical era.

In the election of 1879, the Democrats nominated for governor Louis Wiltz, a long-time ''die-hard Democrat'' leader in New Orleans, and for lieutenant-governor, Samuel McEnery, brother of John McEnery. The Republican nominee for governor was Judge Taylor Beattie, who could hardly be expected to attract the most enthusiastic support from black voters. ''A large and quite conservative sugar planter, Beattie happened to be an ex-slaveholder, an ex-Confederate, and an ex-member of the Knights of the White Camellia. His plantation in Lafourche Parish was named 'Dixie.' '' [1] The returns gave Wiltz 74,000 votes to Beattie's 42,500, which was still rather remarkable, considering the fact that there were more black than white voters registered. Such returns would be commonplace thereafter. Wiltz died in October of 1881, leaving the governor's chair to McEnery. McEnery was elected governor in his own right in 1883, thus holding office from 1881 until 1888—years that might be termed the period of classical Bourbonism in Louisiana.

Bourbon power had a number of bases. The first was entirely mechanical, in that party candidates were selected by convention. The New Orleans Ring controlled the delegates to the

1. Hair, *Bourbonism and Agrarian Protest,* p. 105.

Democratic convention from that city, and since delegates were apportioned among the parishes according to total population, a few great planters from parishes with large black populations dominated the Democratic convention even as they had dominated the legislature before the Civil War. Since the Democratic candidates were certain to be elected, under the prevailing system, control of the party's convention carried with it control of the state government.

Providing the financial support necessary for Bourbon politics—and it was not an exorbitant expense—were the lottery and the beneficiaries of the convict-lease system. Lottery profits were considerable. They were so great that Charles Howard could provide the Confederate Memorial Building for New Orleans, contribute generously to the city's Howard Library, finance expedient political campaigns, and still have more than enough left over to make his family rich. When the Metairie Racing Club refused to vote Howard a membership, he bought the track and converted it into a cemetery. In politics, however, Howard seldom made a personal appearance. Instead, he depended upon Major Burke.

Louisiana probably had a convict-lease system before any other state, but after the Civil War, when more and more blacks were sent to the penitentiary for misdeeds that would only have brought a lashing in slavery days, leasing convicts became big business. One S. L. James became the main contractor for such leases, and others who wished to use convict labor dealt with James. He paid approximately ten cents a day per man. There was no incentive for lessees to treat the prisoners well, because the courts constantly provided new prisoners. Board members charged with overseeing the system received their salaries from the lessees and never reported anything critical. Yet in 1882, 149 out of 700 prisoners died; in 1884, 118 out of 850 died. Governor McEnery insisted that the convicts were "well taken care of, humanely treated, well fed and clothed, and not overtasked in their labor." [2]

Another base of Bourbon power was the regular Democratic

2. Quoted in Hair, *Bourbonism and Agrarian Protest*, p. 131.

political organization, usually known as "the Ring," in New Orleans. New Orleans politics had been redolent of fraud and corruption long before the Civil War, and the practitioners of stuffing ballot boxes, voting people dead and yet unborn, intimidating opponents, and making false returns honed their skills during Reconstruction. The Ring usually had opposition, but it was nearly always victorious. To a remarkable degree, it was a continuation of the old White League organization. It must be emphasized that the Ring did not represent the business interests of New Orleans. On the contrary, its leaders were self-made men, and in general their sympathies lay with the working-class people who, after all, provided their votes.

The "reform" element in New Orleans was usually led by the more prominent businessmen in the city—characteristic of one of the seeming paradoxes in Louisiana politics. Reform in an economic and social sense in Louisiana has generally been carried out by politicians who practically always condone a degree of political corruption and who not infrequently have looked the other way when financial corruption occurred. Louisiana "reformers," on the other hand, have opposed political and financial corruption, but the reforms they have advocated have been administrative. Social and economic reforms have been opposed or at best neglected.

Major Burke must be considered separately as a power base of Bourbonism. As state treasurer, he wielded great power; he could decide whose warrants would be refused, thus forcing those refused to discount their warrants at a bank. He was editor-publisher of one of the most powerful newspapers in the South. Finally, he was at the center of the alliance of the Bourbon politicians, the New Orleans Ring, the lessees of state convicts, and the lottery. He was without a doubt the most powerful man in the state from 1879 to 1888.

By election time in 1887, the voters of Louisiana had become increasingly dissatisfied with the McEnery-Burke-lottery government, although that did not mean that they were ready to support a Republican. The only way to stop McEnery's bid for a second full term was to take the nomination away from him at the Democratic state convention, and to do that, a strong candidate would have to enter the contest. Such a candidate appeared in the person of Francis T. Nicholls, the lottery's arch foe of the late 1870s.

The McEnery-Burke forces campaigned on the race issue. Nicholls was too honest to deal with the Negro question, it was asserted, whereas McEnery knew how to handle bad Negroes, presumably because he was not over-honest. It was even suggested by one McEnery speaker that Nicholls had to be stupid, otherwise he would not have been wounded so often during the Civil War! It was soon evident that Nicholls would control the delegations from the farmer parishes and that, as usual, McEnery would control the plantation-parish delegations. New Orleans would have the deciding voice in the Democratic convention.

In New Orleans, the Ring had come into bad repute. J. Valsin Guillotte had become mayor in 1884 as the result of an election characterized by the usual fraud. Guillotte's appointee as chief of police was shot by a woman he had seduced with the aid of a forged marriage certificate, but he survived to be sentenced to fourteen years in prison. Criminal Sheriff Robert Brewster was killed when he and the Orleans Parish Tax Collector attempted to horsewhip a newspaper editor. The most sensational murder of that period was the killing of one "Cap" Murphy by seven men, one of them Thomas J. Ford, a city judge. Under such circumstances, the Ring was unable to control a majority of the city's delegates to the state Democratic Convention, and Nicholls won the nomination.

Ordinarily, that would have been the end of the matter, since the Republican Party had been reduced to impotence. McEnery, however, did not take defeat gracefully. He announced that as governor he would see to it that the upcoming election was an honest election. That apparently unexceptionable announcement brought consternation to the ranks of Nicholl's supporters. Louisiana still had more black than white voters registered, and if the planters took Governor McEnery at his word and allowed their black sharecroppers to vote as they wished, then the Republican nominee, who happened to be the almost everlasting Henry Clay Warmoth, might very well be elected. After any number of conferences between representatives of the governor and the governor-elect, an agreement seemingly was reached. In the election, 137,000 votes were counted for Nicholls, 52,000 for Warmoth. After he had become governor for the second time, Nicholls appointed McEnery to a seat on the state supreme court.

Nicholls had one advantage upon taking office. Major Burke had gone down to defeat with McEnery and was no longer a power in Louisiana politics. There had been rumors of irregularities in the treasurer's office during the 1887 campaign, and subsequent developments certainly confirmed them. Burke soon left for Europe, and when it became apparent that he was not planning to return, an examination of his accounts was begun. The audit showed him to be the prince among redeemer thieves in the post-Reconstruction South; his books showed a shortage of $1,267,905. Burke eventually settled in Honduras, where he became a leading figure politically and economically, entertaining distinguished visitors from the United States, including Theodore Roosevelt and William McKinley.

For the small farmers of Louisiana, economic and social conditions grew worse with each passing year. In the 1870s, a few farmers in Louisiana had joined the Grange, and a few had adhered to the Greenback Party during its short life. It was most difficult, however, for Louisiana farmers to vote other than Democratic, because in their minds the Democratic party had saved the state from the unbearable evils of "black" Reconstruction. Bourbon politicians convinced them all too easily that a vote against the nominee of the Democratic convention was a vote for a return to Negro rule. Obviously that was not true, since Negro rule had never existed, but farmers, like other people, acted upon their beliefs, not upon the basis of historical fact. Basically, their racism was stronger than the economic interests they shared with black sharecroppers.

As the ravages of a depression that began in 1873 continued, farmers became more and more convinced that they must do something to help themselves. Almost spontaneously, a number of farmers' organizations made their appearance in North Louisiana. The most important was the Farmers' Union, established by John Tetts in Lincoln Parish in 1881. Developments of this kind in Louisiana were not in isolation; farmers were reacting the same way in other southern states and in the Middle West. As a part of the Farmers' Alliance movement, the union was united with other farmers over the South and the Middle West. A Colored Farmers' Alliance in Louisiana had many members, especially in the Red River Valley. By 1890 there may have been twenty thousand members of the White Farmers' Union in Louisiana, but they were concentrated in North Louisiana and the Florida Parishes. In South Louisiana, much less progress was made, largely because the Catholic Church opposed the organization. Apparently, because many of the leaders of the Farmers' Union were also members of the Masonic Order, the Catholic clergy tended to make no distinction between the two.

The main effort of the Farmers' Union in Louisiana was turned toward self-help, in this respect following the earlier pattern of the Grange. A central store was established in New Orleans, to sell goods retail to farmers who shipped their produce to it and to provide goods wholesale for twenty or more Farmers' Union retail outlets in the state. The central store and most of the retail outlets had failed by 1893; scattered remnants did not survive the financial panic of that year. A more successful arrangement, though not really long-lived, was for a group of farmers belonging to the union to make an agreement with a local merchant to give him all their trade in return for reduced prices.

As time passed, more and more planters, as distinguished from farmers, became members of the Farmers' Union. To what extent that occurred because the planters recognized a kinship of interest or to what extent it was an attempt to take over the organization, one cannot say. What is certain is that planters and even small-town businessmen began to have a greater voice in union affairs. Also it is certain that by the late 1880s Bourbon politicians began to realize that agrarian discontent was a factor that must be taken into account in state politics. Francis T. Nicholls, during his second term (1888–1892) proved as adroit in maneuvering the farmers into his wing of the Democratic party as he had been in maneuvering Radical Republicans out of power in 1877.

Some members of the Farmers' Union felt that their ends could never be attained within the Democratic party of Louisiana and joined the People's party, better known as the Populists, which was formed at a convention in Cincinnati, Ohio, in 1891. The movement toward Populism in Louisiana was encouraged by Hardy Brian of Winn Parish, who published and edited the *Winnfield Comrade*. Lest the name of Brian's paper be thought to show Marxist influence, it must be pointed out that he bought the type of the defunct *Winn Parish Democrat*. The only title-size type was that of the previous paper, and Brian shifted the letters about to make up the name *Comrade*. The Populist party quickly gathered strength in the farmer parishes of North Louisiana and in the parishes on or near the Texas line, but ominously it made no inroads into South Louisiana.

Nationally the Populist party made its greatest impression in the election of 1892, when it ran a strong third. In Louisiana the Populist candidate for governor in that year ran last among five candidates. The election demonstrated that the Populist base was entirely too small; their candidate ran ahead in only four hill parishes, and in New Orleans, where the party had no commissioners at the polls, he got only seventy-one votes. Obviously, Populists alone could not break Bourbon control of Louisiana, and the only meaningful alliance would be with the Republicans.

Anti-Democratic sentiment in Louisiana grew by leaps and bounds between 1892 and 1896. Another depression that began in 1893 quickly dropped cotton prices below five cents a pound, well under the cost of production. The price of sugar also dropped, and then, in the Wilson-Gorham Act, the Cleveland administration did away with a two-cent-a-pound bounty on Louisiana sugar and substituted an ad valorem tariff that gave little protection. Thus, the stage was set for co-operation between the wealthy but discontented sugar planters of the South and the poor and discontented cotton farmers of the North. After much negotiation, a "fusion" between Populists and Republicans was effected. John N. Pharr, a millionaire Republican, lumberman, and sugar planter from St. Mary Parish, became the Fusion candidate for governor against Murphy J. Foster, who ran for re-election as the regular Democratic nominee. Pharr was no cynic; despite his wealth, he seems to have believed in Populist principles to some extent and to have been committed completely to honest government. Though he undoubtedly believed in white supremacy, he had never engaged in the race-baiting rhetoric of the era. His money was most useful in financing the Fusion campaign.

The Bourbon Democrats for the first time since Reconstruction faced the very real possibility of defeat. They made no bones of the fact that they would take whatever steps necessary to prevent such a blow to their conception of good government. A Shreveport newspaper professed horror at the fact that the Populists "even go so far as to say that they are in favor of voting the Negro honestly." [3] Planters in the river parishes were horrified to find their sharecroppers, long apathetic, seeking to register so that they might vote the Populist ticket. The Bourbon newspapers made it clear that they would resort to any means to prevent a Populist victory. "It is the religious duty of Democrats to rob Populists and Republicans of their votes whenever and wherever the opportunity presents itself. . . . The Populists and Republicans are our legitimate political prey. Rob them! You bet! What are we here for?" [4] A number of papers including the official state organ, the *Baton Rouge Daily Advocate,* suggested that if the Populists should win the election a bloody conservative revolution would be in order.

As it happened, a right-wing revolution was not necessary; robbery and intimidation proved sufficient. The official count in April 1896 gave Foster 116,116 and Pharr 87,698. However, if those parishes with the largest proportion of black to white pop-

3. *Shreveport Evening Judge,* August 9, 1895: quoted in Hair, *Bourbonism and Agrarian Protest,* p. 249.

4. *Shreveport Evening Judge,* December 15, 1895: quoted in Hair, *Bourbonism and Agrarian Protest,* p. 255.

ulation are omitted from the count, Pharr had a majority despite obvious frauds in New Orleans. Once more the alluvial-parish planters had counted the votes of their sharecroppers as they desired them counted. The strongest reform movement in Louisiana since Reconstruction had been checked, and basic changes in Louisiana politics were delayed for another generation. The Bourbons had been frightened, however, and they determined insofar as possible to eliminate the black vote and in so doing to reduce the voting strength of poor and uneducated whites. The farmers, exhausted by defeat, basically racist, and aware that black votes defeated them, acquiesced.

The newly elected legislature called for an election to determine whether a constitutional convention should meet in 1898 and, if so, to elect delegates. The constitution drawn up by the convention was to go into effect without being referred to the voters. Fewer than eight thousand votes were cast against the convention, and only one Populist delegate was elected. Thus, under the provision of the call, the Bourbon delegates had the power to devise and put into effect any sort of constitution that they might choose.

The constitution that came out of that convention threw some scraps to the Populists. To regulate railroads and utilities, it created a railroad commission (later to become the Public Service Commission); and a stronger state Department of Agriculture and Immigration was formed. Also, the legislature was authorized to set up a state primary system for party nominations if it so chose. The delegates dared offer these concessions because of the restrictions they placed upon voting. Residence requirements remained at two years in the state, one in the parish, and six months in the precinct, which eliminated those sharecroppers who demonstrated independence by moving each year. More important, a voter, to qualify, had to demonstrate the ability to read either English or his native tongue, or he had to possess property assessed at three hundred dollars or more. These provisions were aimed primarily at black voters, of course, but Louisiana had the highest rate of white illiteracy of any state in the Union, and few of the farms belonging to yeomen were assessed at more than three hundred dollars. Added to the requirements was the payment of a poll tax of one dollar per year, and a voter had to present receipts for two years' payment of the poll tax when he appeared at the polls. It was assumed by the men who drafted this section of the constitution that whites would be more likely than blacks to pay their poll tax in years when there was no election, and that blacks who did pay their poll tax would be more likely than whites to misplace their receipts.

The literacy and property requirements would have eliminated a large number of the white voters of Louisiana, but an ingenious escape hatch was provided: a man could register to vote without meeting the literacy or property requirement if he, his father, or his grandfather had been a registered voter in 1867, the last year before Radical Reconstruction began. To make certain that illiterates knew which party they were voting for, the law required that a "device" be placed above the column of candidates for each party. The rooster was selected as the Democratic symbol, and "voting the rooster" became the accepted way of upholding the Democratic party and white supremacy.

The makers of the Constitution of 1898 accomplished what they intended to accomplish. Black-voter registration, which had been 130,000 on January 1, 1897, was reduced to 5,320 on March 17, 1900, and to 1,342 in 1904. Thus, for all practical purposes, black citizens were eliminated from participation in politics. At the same time, white registration was reduced from 164,000 on January 1, 1897, to 125,000 on March 17, 1900, and to 92,000 for the presidential election of 1904. Admittedly, registration in 1896 had been unusually heavy; but even so, a substantial reduction in white registration had been achieved. Obviously, many of the white voters who no longer bothered to register and vote were the poor farmers who had voted for the Fusion ticket in 1896. The planters and the New Orleans machine had achieved a complete victory—so complete that they could afford the luxury of disagreement among themselves, to some extent. Beneath the surface, however, the fires of discontent still smoldered, ready to flare hotter than ever, once they broke into the open. The appearance of a charismatic leader in later years would fan the conflagration.

10

The Beginnings of Change: 1900 to 1924

THE years from 1900 to 1924 in Louisiana saw both the continuation of Bourbon rule—with some variations—and the beginning of a trickle of change. Change was not merely political; the beginning of exploitation of the state's mineral resources presaged far greater change for the future. A new attitude toward education led at long last to the beginning of a reasonably good public school system, at least for the more fortunate among white children. Also a new wave of labor militancy appeared, especially in the lumbering areas of Southwest Louisiana, which combined with the remnants of Populism to produce a remarkable degree of localized radicalism. Basically, Louisiana was playing its part in the national Progressive movement, but the reforms did not come soon enough, nor did they go far enough, to prevent the rise to power of Huey Long.

The elimination of black voters reduced the power of Louisiana's planters, so that the conservatives in Louisiana politics were much more dependent upon the New Orleans Ring for retention of power. In fact, from 1900 to 1920, the Choctaw Club, as the Crescent City organization was usually called, was the single most powerful voice in state politics. The new businessmen of Louisiana, owners of lumber mills, and representatives of the great oil companies and of Union Sulphur Company, were growing in importance, and they were definitely a part of the conservative alliance. They were not bothered by corruption in state government; on the contrary, they were willing to contribute to corruption, if by so doing they could prevent state regulation and, above all, taxation of the interests they represented. It should be added that many New Orleans businessmen, already heavily taxed and poorly governed by the Choctaw Club and its allies, were not a part of this alliance. On the contrary, effective opposition to these latter-day Bourbons was led by New Orleans business and professional men until Huey Long appeared. The opposition group should not, however, be thought of as liberals in either a social or an economic sense. They were willing to improve public services, especially schools, but their primary concern was honest and economical government. They had some allies in the smaller cities of Louisiana, but these small-town businessmen came more and more under the influence of the northern corporations entering the state.

In the meantime, changes taking place in Louisiana's economy were to have far-reaching consequences. The state's lumber industry was at its height early in the twentieth century, but too soon it exhausted the best timber and moved on. Deposits of sulphur had been discovered in Calcasieu Parish during Reconstruction, but they lay deep beneath the surface and could not be profitably mined. The development of the Frasch method of sulphur mining, whereby the sulphur was melted underground and then pumped to the surface as a liquid, made it possible for the Union Sulphur Company to make huge profits through its practical monopoly of production in Louisiana and Texas. The town of Sulphur grew up around the Calcasieu Parish mine. Other sulphur deposits were discovered in Louisiana and in the Gulf of Mexico off the Louisiana coast as the twentieth century wore on.

It was known before the Civil War that there were large salt deposits along the coast of south-central Louisiana. During the war, mines on Avery Island produced salt badly needed by the Confederacy until a Northern raid destroyed the primitive facilities. After the war several attempts at commercial production failed; but finally, in 1898, a successful salt-mining operation began and has continued to the 1970s.

Natural gas was discovered by a man drilling a water well at Shreveport during Reconstruction, and the gas was actually used for a time for lighting at least one building. The discovery was not followed up, however. After drilling for oil began, it was not unusual for gas to be discovered, but for years this valuable resource was burned away as a nuisance. In 1916 a gas field far more extensive than any previously found was brought in near Monroe, and commercial production began. For years natural gas was the cleanest and most economical source of fuel available, and Louisiana was abundantly blessed with reserves. As the last quarter of the twentieth century dawned, however, it became evident that the state's reserves would not last forever and that they might be exhausted in a relatively few years.

Petroleum, of course, would be the chief mineral product of the early twentieth century. The first Louisiana oil well was brought in near Jennings, on land belonging to Jules Clement, in 1901. By 1950, all but a few parishes in the state were producing oil to some extent. Oil and gas would come to be the state's most important source of revenue. Some Lousianians made great fortunes, and others earned good wages, but most of the profits from Louisiana oil production went to northern corporations, and few Louisianians owned stock in these corporations.

In 1909, the Louisiana petrochemical industry began when the Standard Oil Corporation decided to build a refinery at Baton Rouge. Before that, Louisiana had merely pumped oil out of the state for treatment elsewhere. Crude oil could, of course, reach Baton Rouge by rail and by water, but it was also decided to lay an eight-inch pipeline from Oklahoma to assure a steady flow of crude. The refinery, built just north of Baton Rouge on a tract of land that had been set aside as an industrial park, attracted dozens of other industries, not all of them directly connected with petroleum. By 1911 the refinery had a daily capacity of more than seven thousand barrels of oil and was by far the most important employer in the Baton Rouge area.

In 1912, another wave of radicalism washed over much of Louisiana. The Good Government League of New Orleans might have seemed part of that radical movement, but actually it was not; rather, it was a reform movement led by middle-class business and professional men opposed to machine politics. The radicalism of 1912 was Socialist- and labor-oriented, and it was strongest in the old Populist strongholds of North Louisiana and in the lumber camps of Southwest Louisiana. Since the turn of the century, discontent had grown in the lumber camps—typical company towns, completely dominated by the mill owners, who were in a highly competitive business with every incentive to keep wages down. Wages were truly low, ranging perhaps from $10.00 a week for skilled and experienced men to as low as $2.50 a week for those at the least-skilled jobs. Figures do not express real wages, however, because the workers often were paid in scrip, which could be used at face value only in a company store.

Under those conditions, it is not surprising that the timber workers, who made up 60 percent of the industrial workers in Louisiana at the turn of the century, were dissatisfied. Sporadic strikes resulted in the mill owners' forming the Southern Lumber Operators' Association, with headquarters at St. Louis. The association's avowed object was the prevention of effective union organization of lumber workers. If one owner's plant was closed by a strike, he would be granted compensation by an assessment upon other members. Thus the owners were prepared when Arthur L. Emerson and Joey Smith began organizing the Brotherhood of Timber Workers in 1910. Yellow-dog contracts, a partial lockout, and the hiring of strike breakers were successful employer tactics. The lumber workers were definitely losing their battle.

At a union convention at Alexandria in 1912, the delegates heard speeches by William D. (Big Bill) Haywood and Covington Hall, of the truly radical International Workers of the World, and enthusiastically voted to affiliate with the IWW. Organization and resistance to it proceeded thereafter at a feverish pace, almost sure to bring violence in a state where it had long been customary to settle serious arguments with a gun. The violence came on July 7, 1912, at the little mill town of Graybow, west of DeRidder. At Graybow, a skirmish broke out when union leaders began making speeches to strikebreakers, and one guard and three union men were killed. Sixty-two union men were arrested, and nine, indicted for murder, were tried and acquitted in October, after almost four months in jail. While the trial was going on, a lockout and then a strike took place at nearby Merryville; that stoppage lasted almost a year. It was in the midst of this turmoil that the presidential election of 1912 took place.

In 1912, Populist remnants and members of the IWW united in support of Eugene V. Debs, the Socialist candidate for president. The Socialists did not carry the state; that was unthinkable with southern-born Woodrow Wilson heading the Democratic ticket. However, one Louisianian out of every fourteen who voted did vote for Debs, who ran ahead of regular Republican William Howard Taft. The Socialists were strongest in exactly those places where the Populists had been strongest in 1896, and in Winn Parish they elected a number of parish officials. Their vote was comparatively heavy in the lumber parishes of Southwest Louisiana, but it undoubtedly would have been higher if so many lumber workers had not been transients, prevented from voting by either residence requirements, the poll tax, or both.

Socialist radicalism declined as rapidly as it had risen, but twice the farmers of North Louisiana and the workers and farmers of Southwest Louisiana had demonstrated that they could respond to a radical call. The call would come again in 1924 and again, ever more strongly, in 1928. Huey Long was twenty-one when the Socialists carried Winn Parish in 1912. Certainly he and his younger brother Earl were not Socialists, but it seems plausible that Huey's call for sharing the wealth and Earl's determination to create a welfare state can be traced in some degree to Socialist voices heard in their youth.

Governors who owed their election to the Ring were not completely oblivious to the Progressive movement. Under Governor William Heard (1900–1904), the convict-lease system came to an end, for all practical purposes. Under Governor Newton Blanchard (1904–1908), the convention system of nominations came to an end, and the primary became the means of nominating almost all party candidates for office. In what had become a one-party state, the primary gave the voters a far greater voice in choosing public officials. On the other hand, the primary fastened the one-party system on the state more securely than ever. The primary was restricted to registered Democrats, and the voter who listed himself as a Republican was removing himself from meaningful participation in the political process.

The greatest strides were made in education. Under Blanchard, appropriations for public schools increased from $1.5 million in 1904 to $3.5 million in 1908. That made it possible for 66,000 more children to be enrolled, but the school system was still far from adequate. Terms were short, teachers were inadequately trained and grossly underpaid, and despite improvements, tens of thousands of children had no opportunity at all to attend school. That was especially true of black children; in very few parishes was there any effort to provide better schools for them. Even so, the public school situation in 1908 was far better than it had been in 1900, and improvements would continue in subsequent years.

Improvements in higher education were even more noteworthy. Among private schools, the University of Louisiana, opened in 1834, became Tulane University in 1884, when it was endowed by Paul Tulane; in 1904, the Jesuit order established Loyola College, chartered in 1912 as Loyola University, in New Orleans; and St. Mary's Dominican College for girls came into being in 1906. In North Louisiana the Baptist Church combined a number of existing schools, including Mount Lebanon University, to create Louisiana College at Pineville. Centenary College, founded in 1825, was moved from Jackson to the thriving city of Shreveport, where it became an outstanding liberal arts college. In the public sector, Louisiana State University was combined with Louisiana Agricultural and Mechanical College, a land-grant institution chartered during Reconstruction, in 1877, and has continued to grow steadily, if slowly. In 1884 Louisiana Normal School was established at Natchitoches with a two-year curriculum; it was converted to a senior college in 1917 and eventually became Northwestern State University. Louisiana Industrial Institute had been established at Ruston in 1895 and eventually became a senior college, later known as Louisiana Polytechnic Institute and, still later, Louisiana Tech University. Louisiana Institute, which would develop into the University of Southwestern Louisiana, came into being in Lafayette in 1901. Southern University had been established by the Constitutional Convention of 1879, but it did not graduate its first student until 1887. As late as 1898 it had only ten students taking college-level courses, but in the twentieth century it became for a time the largest Negro state university in the United States.

In the election of 1908, the Ring candidate, J. Y. Sanders, won the primary and demonstrated that the forces controlling Louisiana state politics for a generation under the convention system would not be automatically displaced by primary mominations. The Good Government League under John M. Parker was established in New Orleans in 1910, and in 1912 the league candidate, Luther Hall, received enough New Orleans votes to win the Democratic nomination. Hall's administration was hamstrung, however, by the fact that a majority of the legislature was opposed to him. In 1916 the Ring returned to power, electing Ruffin G. Pleasant governor over Parker. Probably Pleasant had no desire to effect reforms, but even if he had, a term that encompassed the United States's participation in World War I was no time for new departures on the local scene.

While Pleasant did little in the governor's office, Parker was active. Out of the remains of the Good Government League, he created the strongest anti-Ring organization yet seen in New Orleans. He sought allies for his candidacy among the farmers of North Louisiana, and among those who came out in support of Parker was a young native of Winn Parish named Huey P. Long. When the campaign began, Parker demanded a severance tax on gas and oil, the bringing of cheap natural gas to New Orleans, better schools, better roads, and a better state university. He also insisted on a new constitution, and he promised to end the Choctaw Club's control of the state. Parker organized well, and he campaigned well. When the votes were in, he had 40 percent of the New Orleans vote. That, combined with a sub-

stantial majority in South Louisiana and the hills of North Louisiana, assured him of the Democratic nomination and the governorship in 1920.

Historians must be careful with might-have-beens, but it
seems possible that, despite the failures of reform in the past,
Louisiana might have had the benefits of the Huey Long regime
without the excesses if Parker had had Long's determination,
and perhaps lack of scruple, in pushing his programs through.
He did not have those qualities, however; rather it was his policy in general to stand aside and let nature take its course after
one of his proposals had been introduced into the legislature or,
in some cases, the Constitutional Convention of 1921. The opposition to reform, led by the Ring's representatives, blunted
the reform thrust; Parker's supporters, left without leadership,
floundered to defeat.

Parker sought a moderate tax on the state's industries, which
more and more meant petrochemical industries; but the Ring,
the delta cotton planters, and the business interests defeated
him. He did not fight hard for a graduated income tax, strongly
opposed by wealthier citizens, stating that his preference was
for a flat percentage tax on incomes large and small. He had
more luck with a severance tax on minerals, though he had to
negotiate the amount, eventually 3 percent ad valorem, with
Standard Oil, whose attorneys drafted the bill. Most of the
money from the severance tax was to be used to support Louisiana State University, which Parker located on a new campus
south of Baton Rouge. The poor people of the state felt that the
public schools should have been built up first, and only then
should so much money have been dedicated to the university.
Parker did bring about the writing and adoption of a new constitution in 1921, and that document brought no great amount of
criticism at the time. In practice, over the next half-century, the
Constitution of 1921, disorganized, confusing, contradictory,
and interminably long, proved first to be a nuisance, then a
joke, and finally an enormity. So many amendments were necessary that, eventually, just before its demise in 1974, it was
well over a thousand pages long.

Without doubt, however, Parker's greatest error was in assenting to a pay-as-you-go plan for improving the state's roads. It should be remembered that in 1921 the Model T had been on the road for thirteen years, and the automobile, whatever the make or model, had become an inseparable part of American life. Yet, except in and around the larger towns in the more prosperous parishes, Louisiana roads were not much better than they had been before the Civil War. Parker has been referred to as the "gravel-road" governor, and he did see to it that gravel or shell was placed on many a mile of state road. But in South Louisiana, the gravel and shell soon sank out of sight in the mud, and in North and South Louisiana, the majority of farmers did not live on state roads, but on parish roads that were just as bad as ever.

Thus Louisiana's chance of reform by gentlemen passed, if ever it had really existed. It has sometimes been said that Huey Long's reforms would have come about without him under the leadership of men like Parker, but that statement ignores the fact that Parker's program was emasculated, if not defeated, by the same forces that opposed Long so bitterly. In the early 1900s, the age of Populism was long past in the United States as a whole, because the small farmer had ceased to be a significant factor in the population. He was still very important in Louisiana, however, and if the vote of the Protestant hill farmers of North Louisiana could be combined with that of the Catholic small farmers of South Louisiana, control of the state could be won. Certainly, however, it was going to take an elemental force to break the bonds of Bourbon conservatism, reinforced by an urban political machine and the political machinations of modern big business, which kept Louisiana's common people, black and white, tied to an unpleasant past. Huey Long would be that elemental force, but he could not be confined to correcting evils. The methods he chose to achieve his ends were such that not a few Louisianians believed that the treatment was worse than the ills it was intended to cure.

11

Bottom Rail on Top: Huey P. Long and the Break with the Past

*H*UEY Pierce Long has often been listed with the southern demagogues, and perhaps he was a true demagogue, the choice of the common people of his state, to a greater extent than James K. Vardaman or Theodore Bilbo of Mississippi, Benjamin Tillman of South Carolina, or James Heflin of Alabama, to name some others who appear on such lists. There was one crucial difference, however, between Long and the stereotyped southern demagogue: Huey P. Long never belabored the race issue, and neither did his brother Earl, who served two full terms and part of a third as governor of Louisiana. In contrast, the Longs came to power with a program designed to bring positive material benefits to the poorer people of the Pelican State, and to a considerable extent their programs were enacted into law. Whether their policies were designed for the purpose of bringing them to power, or whether they sought power as a means of carrying out their policies, is beyond the power of the historian to determine.

It can be stated categorically that the Longs—most especially Huey Long—were the heirs of that strain of protest among farmers and workers of Louisiana that had shown itself with varying intensity in opposition to the Civil War, in the Populist movement, and in the Socialist movement of 1912. Huey Long's opposition was made up of the planters, the New Orleans political machine, and the representatives of business who had opposed Populism and who, although not really threatened, had opposed Socialism. He put an end, apparently for good, to that "government by gentlemen" that had characterized Louisiana politics, except for the Reconstruction interlude, from the colonial beginnings. Opponents who followed the Longs in power had little choice but to maintain the policies that the Longs had instituted.

Huey Long may have been the most remarkable American of the twentieth century. His early death, only seven years after he had come to national attention, leaves the field wide open to speculation as to what he might otherwise have accomplished for good or for evil. He had made himself as near absolute dictator of Louisiana as was possible under a federal system of government, and his ambition had turned to the national scene. His "share-the-wealth" program was definitely attracting a national following, and leaders of the national Democratic party were justifiably concerned with the effect that he might have on the 1936 presidential campaign.

One thing Huey Long did not do was put an end to the corruption so long characteristic of Louisiana politics and government. He himself seems to have been honest, insofar as personal finances were concerned; his appetite was for power, not wealth. On the other hand, he had no more scruples about dishonesty in manipulating the electoral process than his nineteenth-century predecessors had. The men he had gathered around him, once his personal domination was removed, were revealed as a remarkably venal group, affording one of the juiciest series of scandals to be celebrated in the American press in this century.

Huey Long was born in 1893, the next-to-the-youngest of the nine children of Huey Pierce Long, Sr., and Caledonia Tison Long. His birthplace was Winnfield, in Winn Parish, which had opposed secession, had given little and grudging support to the Confederacy, and had been a hotbed of Populist sentiment in the

1890s and of Socialist activity in 1912. Huey Long, Sr., was neither a Populist nor a Socialist, but an intelligent, inquisitive boy growing up in Winnfield could not have avoided frequent and prolonged exposure to the ideas of Louisiana protest.

The Longs were not poor. The senior Huey Long owned more than three hundred acres, free and clear. His prosperity is evidenced by the fact that six of his nine children attended college, something almost unheard-of for the children of a Louisiana farm family in the late nineteenth and early twentieth century. Furthermore, the Longs were readers of books, magazines, and newspapers, and they discussed what they had read. The household most definitely did not suffer from the intellectual malnutrition that poverty and isolation imposed upon so many farm families in the hills of North Louisiana.

Very probably, also, the nine Long children inherited some unusual and perhaps remarkable genetic traits. Of the children, two sons attained the governorship and one became a United States senator and potential candidate for president. Another son was a successful attorney, and still another a dentist and a United States representative. One daughter died in infancy, but the others all achieved at least a two-year normal school diploma. One earned a master's degree at Columbia University and became a college teacher. All in all, it was a talented family; Huey Long, Jr., was only the most remarkable of the group.

Most of Huey Long's formal education was at Winnfield, where he proved his brilliance but was unable to get along with the faculty of the high school and never received a diploma. Most of his education—and it must be emphasized that he was well-educated—came from his reading, from constant interchange of ideas with others, and from his constantly growing understanding of human nature. He worked for some time, successfully, as a salesman of cooking oil, which not only contributed to his understanding of people but also gave him confidence in his powers of persuasion. Not the least important result of his sales career was his meeting and marrying Rose McConnell.

Though successful as a salesman, Huey Long always seems to have felt that he was destined for a political life, and he realized that the law was the best profession for an aspiring politician. His brother Julius, already a successful attorney in Winnfield, encouraged him in his ambition to study law. A legend that refuses to die holds that Huey Long completed the three-year Tulane University law course in one year. That is not true; in fact, because he did not have a high-school diploma, Long was not even eligible for admission to the regular law course. What he did do was enroll as a special student, study diligently for a year, and at the end of that time pass an examination for admission to the bar.

The fledgling lawyer returned to Winnfield to practice as a partner of his brother Julius, but the partnership was short-lived. Apparently the Longs were all so strong-willed that they could not get along with one another. When the partnership was dissolved, Huey's practice would not support his family, so he returned to selling. This time, he sold a container for the kerosene used to fuel the lamps that lighted most homes, and he made enough money at it to keep his law office open. Gradually he began to get more cases, mainly suits by workers against timber companies. No doubt he could have been comfortably successful as an attorney had he chosen to remain in Winnfield. Instead, he moved to Shreveport, where he quickly became prosperous.

In 1918 Long moved into the political arena and became a candidate for membership on the state Railroad Commission. The commission had been established by the Constitution of 1898 to regulate railroads, steamboats, pipelines, and telegraph and telephone companies. It had functioned hardly at all since its establishment, serving more as a refuge for politicians who sought an office with little work and less responsibility. It has been said that Long had no organization for his campaign, but that is not altogether true. The Long family and its many connections were in themselves no mean organization; and in his days as a salesman Long had made friends all over the Third Commission District that he sought to represent.

He had also made lists of candidates who had been elected and those who had been defeated in recent compaigns in the parishes of his district, and he had been making himself known

to them for more than a year before he began formal campaigning. He engaged in what was, for the time and place, a tremendous direct-mail campaign, much of the work handled by his
wife. Also, he campaigned in an automobile. He drove abomi-
nably, but with the car, when roads were passable, he could
reach hamlets never before visited by a candidate for important
office. He tacked posters extolling his virtues to trees, telephone
poles, and other visible spots all over the district. Finally, he
spoke. He spoke to individuals, and he spoke to crowds. He
sold himself as he had earlier sold cooking oil and kerosene
tanks. In the first primary, he ran a close second. In the runoff,
he won nomination for the commission by 675 votes. In the absence of Republican opposition, there was no general election,
and Long took office in December of 1918.

Space permits only a few sentences concerning Long's activities as a member of the Railroad Commission—or the Public
Service Commission, as it was designated in the Louisiana Constitution of 1921. He definitely served the public interest by protecting the people from the rapacity of some corporations, but
he also saw to it that he got the utmost of favorable publicity for
his actions. In the campaign of 1919–1920 he supported Parker
for the governorship, but then publicly and loudly broke with
Governor Parker when attorneys for Standard Oil Company
were permitted to write the bill levying a severance tax on gas,
oil, and other natural resources. He waged a long and ultimately
unsuccessful campaign to bring Standard Oil operations in Louisiana under control of the commission, but he got as much publicity as an opponent of "the interests" as he would have got
had he been victorious. By the end of 1922 it was obvious that
he was a candidate for the governorship in the 1923–1924 election campaign.

In 1924, Long set forth the basic program that would later
take him into office: better roads, better schools, free textbooks
for children, a better court system, and—as a legacy from Populism—state-owned warehouses where farmers could store
their produce while waiting for a better market. He approved the
right of labor to organize, and he opposed the use of injunctions
in labor disputes. He denounced the influence of corporations
upon state government, concentrated wealth in general, and "su-

pergovernment''—a euphemism for the Ku Klux Klan. The second Ku Klux Klan—a nationwide organization that flourished after World War I—had become powerful in North Louisiana and Southwest Louisiana in the early 1920s. It was, of course, anti-Negro, anti-Jewish, and anti-Catholic. The other two candidates denounced the Klan, and Long, who certainly had no sympathy for it, criticized mildly. He tried to campaign by advocating his issues and attacking his opponents. He made statewide use of circulars, and toward the end of the campaign, he began to make speeches on the radio. But the Klan issue was one he could not surmount. When the votes were counted, Long was in third place, less than seven thousand votes behind Henry L. Fuqua, who became governor. But as knowledgeable men analyzed the vote, Long evidently could win the governorship at the next election if he could make even minor gains outside of North Louisiana.

Huey Long's task between 1924 and 1927 was to effect a combination that would bring him enough votes in New Orleans or South Louisiana or both to make a majority when combined with his following from North Louisiana. In the runoff gubernatorial primary of 1924 he supported neither candidate, making no friends, but also making no new enemies. In the nominating primary preceding the national election in the fall of 1924, however, Long threw his support to Joseph E. Ransdell for the United States Senate. Ransdell was a Catholic candidate for the Senate, opposed by a Protestant; and under those circumstances, he was happy to have Long's support and to promise a *quid pro quo* in 1927. Long was well aware that by supporting a Catholic he could create a more favorable attitude toward himself in South Louisiana. Ransdell won, and almost surely he owed his victory to Huey Long.

For Long, there remained the problem of obtaining support in rural South Louisiana. The key to that proved to be the campaign of Edwin Broussard, Catholic, French, a favorite of South Louisianians, who was opposed for renomination to his United States Senate seat by Protestant former governor J. Y. Sanders. Sanders would get enough votes in South Louisiana to win the election unless Broussard garnered votes in North Louisiana—a most uncertain possibility because of his religion and his opposition to prohibition, strongly supported by the hill parishes. Broussard needed help badly, and Long, seeing another profitable alliance in the offing, hurried to provide that support. Here again legend is not quite in accord with fact. The legend is that Long campaigned for Broussard only in the south, thus becoming well-known in South Louisiana, but that, in the northern part of the state, he let nature take its course. It is a fact that Long campaigned strenuously in South Louisiana, but the campaign trails of North Louisiana were not ignored. Broussard won in a very close election, and there can be little doubt that Long's support made the difference. Thus he had another entry to votes that had not been available to him in 1924.

In the gubernatorial campaign of 1928, Long's financial resources were much more nearly adequate for the obvious reason that he had a good chance to win. He denounced his chief opponent, United States Representative Riley Joe Wilson, in traditional fashion, but far more than in 1924 he emphasized the program he himself advocated. He put special emphasis upon his proposal to provide free textbooks for all children, whether they attended public, private, or parochial schools. In South Louisiana, at the village of St. Martinville, near the site of the earliest Acadian settlements in Louisiana, he made perhaps the greatest speech of his life. Standing under the Evangeline Oak, he told his listeners:

> And it is here, under this oak where Evangeline waited for her lover, Gabriel, who never came. This oak is an immortal spot, made so by Longfellow's poem, but Evangeline is not the only one who has waited here in disappointment. Where are the schools that you have waited for your children to have, that have never come? Where are the roads and highways that you send your money to build, that are no nearer now than ever before? Where are the institutions to care for the sick and disabled? Evangeline wept bitter tears in her disappointment, but it lasted through only one lifetime. Your tears in this country, around this oak, have lasted for generations. Give me the chance to dry the tears of those who still weep here! [1]

1. Huey P. Long, *Every Man a King* (New Orleans: National Book Co., Inc., 1933), p. 99.

When the votes cast in the first primary had been counted, it was obvious that Long's bid for a bigger share of the New Orleans vote had failed, and on the night after the election, his opponents held premature celebrations. The next day, with the Ku Klux Klan issue long dead, the North Louisiana vote flooded in overwhelmingly for Long, but that had been expected. What the conservatives had not anticipated was an equally overwhelming pro-Long vote from the rural parishes of South Louisiana. The campaigning for Broussard and appeals like that at the Evangeline Oak had paid off handsomely. Long did not have a full majority in the first primary, but it was obvious to any experienced observer that he was a certain winner in a runoff. Wilson withdrew, and in the absence of Republican opposition, Huey Long was governor-elect of Louisiana. The era of the Kingfish had begun.

Contrary to oft-encountered opinion, it was not with absolute power to do as he pleased that Long entered the Louisiana governor's mansion—which he soon tore down and replaced. He had to bargain hard to get majorities for the measures he wanted, and his enemies were almost able to oust him from office. He did, during his first year, succeed in getting natural gas, which Louisiana had in abundance, piped into New Orleans, much to the benefit of the city's residents and industries. He pushed a relatively small bond issue for road and bridge construction through the legislature in the form of a constitutional amendment that still had to be approved by a majority of voters. Certainly roads and bridges were needed. Estimates vary, but the state had only about 300 miles of paved roads when Long took office. There was no bridge across the Mississippi south of Memphis, though one was completed at Vicksburg during Long's governorship. When his term ended, there were 1,583 miles of paved road with much more being built, and bridges over the Mississippi at Baton Rouge and New Orleans had been authorized; they would be completed under his successors. The roadbuilding program he began had not yet come to a halt in 1976, though perhaps the time had come.

Among his earlier accomplishments, Long took most pride in the distribution of free textbooks. That program undoubtedly made it possible for some children who otherwise could not have attended school to do so. It was financed by a severance tax on natural resources in general and natural gas and petroleum in particular. Children in parochial schools benefitted as much as those in public schools, and nothing Long ever did bound the Creoles and Acadians of South Louisiana to him more firmly. To the constitutional argument that the state could not provide aid to parochial schools, he had a ready reply. The distribution of free textbooks did not aid parochial schools; the aid was to the children attending those schools.

In getting his programs enacted, Long extended his control of patronage as much as a sometimes hostile legislature would permit, well aware that he would need all the leverage he could get if he was to continue to get his proposals enacted into law. In the spring of 1929 he overestimated his control of the legislature—or perhaps the ability of his followers to resist temptation—and called a special session of the lawmakers to increase the tax on oil production. The oil companies in general, and Standard Oil Company in particular, reacted quickly to this proposal, and a veritable army of lobbyists descended upon Baton Rouge. The president of Standard Oil of Louisiana, with apparently unlimited funds at his disposal, took over a floor in the little city's major hotel and became the director of opposition to the governor. When the anti-Long bloc began to demonstrate real power, some men who had been the governor's followers for years began to desert what appeared to be a losing cause.

In a highly disorderly session, the Louisiana House of Representatives eventually adopted seven articles of impeachment. However, only one of those articles was adopted before April 6, the date set for adjournment of the special session. The senate by majority vote rejected that article. The governor's defenders argued that the articles adopted after April 6 had no validity. The senate, by a majority of one, refused to accept that argument, but the closeness of the vote revealed that conviction was impossible. Before the trial was under way, fifteen senators signed a statement of their conviction that the articles of impeachment were invalid, wherefore they would refuse to vote to convict, no matter what evidence was presented. Since the senate had thirty-nine members, the futility of further proceedings was evident to all. Long always admitted, and paid more than once, his debt to those fifteen men.

The impeachment may be looked upon as a turning point in Huey Long's political career. His personality did not change, and he had sometimes been as ruthless before the spring of 1929 as he was afterward, but afterward he was much more likely to go for the jugular of those who opposed him. More than ever he was convinced that the ends he sought to achieve were so important that he was justified in using any available means to achieve them. It cannot be denied that his accomplishments for the people of Louisiana were many. While he controlled the state, and he continued to do so until his death, even though he was serving as United States senator, the poll tax was repealed, a graduated income tax was adopted, and homestead exemptions were granted. The last-named exempted homesteads from ad valorem property taxes levied by state and parish governments, with the result that most Louisiana homeowners paid no state or parish taxes on their homes.

The support of Charity Hospital in New Orleans was greatly increased; and under Long's successors, plans for tearing down the old hospital building and erecting a new one were carried out. A medical school of Louisiana State University was established in New Orleans to add to the state's supply of physicians. Larger appropriations were provided for the state's public schools, black as well as white, though at the cost of politicizing the system. In fairness, however, it should be noted that the public schools were not free of politics before or after Huey Long The state colleges also benefitted from the state's new generosity, and Long sought to make Louisiana State University at Baton Rouge into a great institution of learning. Like many of the school's alumni, he had a lamentable tendency to equate greatness with a winning football team, but the academic departments shared in his bounty (and his politics), and sound progress was made in teaching and scholarship.

In 1930 Long ran against and defeated former ally Joseph E. Ransdell for a seat in the United States Senate. He could not enter into his new office immediately, however, because Louisiana's Lieutenant Governor Paul Cyr had become one of his bitterest enemies. When Cyr lost patience and had himself sworn in as governor, on the grounds that the governorship was vacant, Long declared the lieutenant-governorship vacant, and he was in time upheld by the courts. When Long finally did take the oath as United States senator, Alvin King, president of the Louisiana Senate, became governor for the short time remaining in the term.

In the United States Senate Long quickly became a national figure. He had backed Franklin D. Roosevelt for the Democratic nomination in 1932 and had campaigned for Roosevelt vigorously and effectively. He soon broke with the president and the national Democratic party, however, and began, in effect, campaigning for the presidency in 1936. The country was in the grip of the Great Depression that had begun in 1929, and millions of people were ready to listen to new and radical proposals. Long advocated what he called the "share-the-wealth" plan, under which great fortunes would be confiscated to the extent necessary to give every head of household five thousand dollars. Probably the plan was as impractical as opponents asserted, but it rapidly gained adherents from one end of the nation to the other.

There can be no doubt that the Roosevelt administration, presumably with the president's approval, set out to "get" Long. The use of the Internal Revenue Service to punish political enemies of a national administration did not begin in the 1970s. It has been asserted that Long would have been indicted had he not been murdered; but the Kingfish's chief biographer maintains that there is no substance to this assertion.[2] Also, of course, indictment is one thing; conviction is another. But Long was well aware that Washington was watching his every step. Because of his presidential aspirations and probably because of the hostility of the national administration, Long needed a secure power base in Louisiana.

Unfortunately, like many other strong men, Huey Long had

2. T. Harry Williams, *Huey Long* (New York: Alfred A. Knopf, 1969), pp. 826–828.

few other strong men about him; indeed, the word *pliant* applies to most of his associates. At least from 1929 on, Long concentrated more and more power in his own hands. Perhaps he felt that he was justified in using dubious, even patently illegal, methods to get centralizing measures on the statute books because of the nature of his opposition and because he believed that he represented the true interests of the people of Louisiana. Before the end, however, he almost certainly thirsted for power for the sake of power. Perhaps of all great Americans he affords the best example of the truth of Lord Acton's dictum that "Power tends to corrupt; absolute power corrupts absolutely."

The end came in September of 1935. Senator Long ordered a special session of the Louisiana legislature, and one of his objects was to gerrymander judicial districts so as to eliminate Judge Benjamin Pavy, and anti-Long judge so popular that he had been in office for twenty-eight years. On the evening of Sunday, September 8, 1935, Huey Long had come to the new skyscraper state capitol that he had had built and had gone into conference with his legislative leaders. As Senator Long walked down a hall toward the governor's office, he met Dr. Carl D. Weiss, Judge Pavy's son-in-law, and extended his arm for the politician's handshake. Weiss fired one shot at pointblank range before Long's bodyguards shot him to shreds. The bullet from a small Belgian gun passed through Long's kidney and intestines, inflicting a wound which, at that stage of medical knowledge, was probably mortal, though the surgeon who operated failed to realize that the kidney had been injured. On Tuesday, September 10, Huey Long died.

The five years that followed Huey Long's death have been referred to as the "Louisiana Hayride," a title taken from a popular song. Probably, though not certainly, it was the most scandal-ridden period of Louisiana history. Interestingly enough, the opportunities for theft on a large scale came about because Long's successors quickly made peace with the Roosevelt administration in Washington. Federal money flowed into Louisiana as New Deal agencies distributed their largesse. The opportunities for loot were too much for the weak men whom Huey Long had left in power. It should be added, however, that

Richard W. Leche, who became governor in 1936 and who went to the penitentiary, had not been Long's choice for that office, but rather was the choice of Robert Maestri, by that time political boss of New Orleans with Long's blessing. On the other hand, James Monroe Smith, the feckless president of Louisiana State University who speculated in the commodity market and lost hundreds of thousands of dollars he had raised by issuing fraudulent LSU bonds, *had* been Long's choice. In addition to these two men, a half dozen or so others went to jail on one charge or another, most often evasion of federal income tax or using the mails to defraud. Some others committed suicide. The "Hayride" made front pages all over the United States, and the impression was left in many minds that the Huey Long era had brought corruption to Louisiana. Those who gained that impression had forgotten, or had never known, that corruption had been the fashion in Louisiana since before the Civil War. It is certainly possible that, if it had not been for the zeal of federal prosecutors, there would have been few indictments and no convictions. Certainly there would not have been so many. The scandals were not an aberration in Louisiana history. The aberration came before the scandals, as Huey Long gained and consolidated power.

Without question, Long represents the watershed of Louisiana history. What the Jacksonians, the Radical Republicans, the Populists, and the Socialists had failed to do, Huey Long accomplished. He put an end to government by "gentlemen" who, when not corrupt, were concerned only with preserving their own position, status, and wealth and that of others like them. There can be little doubt that even the worst manifestations of Longism represented the will of the people of Louisiana. In view of what had gone before, Huey Long or someone like him was a necessity if Louisiana was ever to come out of the nineteenth century and into the twentieth. But however necessary his actions, his methods became more and more reprehensible. Perhaps, when it came, his death was as essential as his life had been.

12

Recent Louisiana:
The Sweep of Change

LIKE most of the world, Louisiana has seen more change since the beginning of World War II than ever before in history. The way of life of all Louisianians has been affected to greater or lesser degree. The Pelican State remained unique, but it succumbed to much of the standardization brought by the automobile, radio, the war, and television. The quality of life was altered, in the hills of North Louisiana and along the bayous in the south, but whether changes were for good or ill depended upon the point of view of the observer.

In politics, the state remained for many years polarized into Longs and anti-Longs. Largely as a result of the scandals, anti-Long forces led by Sam Jones won control of the state government in 1940 and retained control for eight years. To win again, in 1944, they had to rely on the appeal of country-music singer and composer Jimmy Davis, who drew many votes that might have gone to the Long candidate. During the Jones administration (1940–1944), statutes that had given the governor additional powers were repealed, a civil service system was established, and some administrative reforms were attempted. Jones made no effort to do away with the social measures instituted by Huey Long; in fact, he increased taxes slightly in order to improve the school hot-lunch program and to increase old-age pensions. The Davis administration (1944–1948) did nothing of note, though the fact that it came into office in the midst of World War II was perhaps mainly responsible for inaction.

In 1948, after one of the hardest-fought campaigns in modern Louisiana history, Earl Long defeated Sam Jones for the governorship. It was Earl Long's second administration; as lieutenant governor, he had succeeded to the governorship on Richard Leche's resignation in 1939. After his election in 1948, Earl Long took giant steps toward a welfare state. Old-age pensions were raised to fifty dollars per month; charity hospital services were expanded to include free ambulance service, and provision was made for free beds in private hospitals in areas distant from a charity hospital. Free dental clinics were set up in trailers travelling over the state. Appropriations for the hot-lunch program in the schools were increased fourfold; teachers' salaries were raised, and the salaries of black and white teachers were equalized. More money was provided for road-building, and grants were made to the parishes for the improvement of roads under their jurisdiction.

Obviously, these programs cost money. The sales tax was increased, and specific tax increases were levied on gasoline, beer, and cigarettes. Certainly of benefit to the state were increased taxes on natural gas and petroleum taken from Louisiana wells. Money was not the only cost: patronage was needed to gain the legislative majority for some controversial items, and the civil sevice system was abolished everywhere except in New Orleans; the Crescent City was excepted because anti-Long forces were in control of the city's government.

In 1952 Robert F. Kennon, a very conservative North Louisiana judge, won the governorship. His chief accomplishment was the restoration of civil service. Kennon won not so much because of dissatisfaction with Earl Long's policies, but because the national civil rights movement had begun to impinge upon Louisiana state politics; race was becoming an issue again, a half century after the Constitution of 1898 had supposedly laid the question to rest forever. When Huey Long became governor in 1928, fewer than a thousand Louisiana blacks were registered to vote, but during the 1930s, black people in Louisiana, as elsewhere, transferred their loyalty from the Republican to the

Democratic party. Beginning in the 1940s, the number of Louisiana blacks on the registration lists began in increase, especially in New Orleans and South Louisiana, and those voters tended to support Long candidates. In 1948 Earl Long and his nephew, United States Senator Russell Long, had remained loyal to the Democratic party after it took a strong stand on civil rights at its national convention. Most Louisianians favored the States Rights, or Dixiecrat, party formed by dissident southerners, and Kennon was a strong Dixiecrat.

In 1956 Earl Long won a majority in the first primary, but his third administration was not so successful as his second. The chief political issue on the minds of most Louisianians was race. That had come about as a result of the United States Supreme Court's decision declaring segregation in the schools illegal. Governor Long was loyal to the national Democratic party, and he also was well aware that most Louisiana Negroes had supported him. Thus in those North Louisiana parishes where blacks had been permitted to register, Long opposed efforts to remove their names from the voting rolls. At that crucial time, he apparently suffered a nervous breakdown.

The next few months were a nightmare for Louisianians who valued the dignity of their state and a tragedy for Earl Long. Pursued by a pack of reporters, he was hurried to a mental institution in Texas, from whence he was quickly released when it became evident that due process had been ignored. Back in Louisiana, he was taken to a state hospital in Mandeville. There he became aware of what was happening, if he had ever been unaware, and he used his authority as governor to fire the director of the hospital, appointing a physician who knew where the power lay. Released from confinement, Long soon took a trip to Texas and across the border to Juarez, in Mexico, pursued always by reporters. On one occasion, apparently hoping to discourage photographers, he put a pillowcase over his head; the resulting picture appeared all over the world. It has been suggested that the chief evidence of the governor's mental incapacity, as seen by Louisiana politicians, was that he made a speech to the legislature opposing the denial of voting rights to black people. When his term expired he ran unsuccessfully for lieutenant governor, but then was elected to Congress from his home district in the fall national elections. He died before he could take office.

The elections of 1960 and 1964 were throwbacks to the time of the Bourbons. In the first primary in 1960 an old-line segregationist, mouthing the slogans that demagogues in other southern states had used for almost a century, ran an unexpectedly strong race, though he did not get into the second primary. The candidates in the runoff were DeLesseps S. Morrison, reform mayor of New Orleans, and former governor Jimmie Davis. Morrison had the public image of a moderate on the race question, which had become an especially emotional issue because of court-ordered integration of a New Orleans school. Davis, who had been very cautious on race in the first primary, became an all-out segregationist in the runoff, and he defeated Morrison easily.

There ensued one of the most unattractive periods in Louisiana history. Presumably members of the legislature, many of them lawyers, knew that the United States government could not be defied by a single state or, since 1865, by a section of states. Yet the legislature, at the governor's call, remained in one special session after another for months, attempting in one way or another to evade what had become the law of the land. All such measures failed, of course, and the integration of schools proceeded slowly but inexorably. The issue remained alive, however, and was used successfully in 1964 by John J. McKeithen, who defeated DeLesseps Morrison, in what turned out to be Morrisons's last try for office before his death in a plane crash. McKeithen was powerful enough during his first term to suceed in getting ratified a constitutional amendment permitting him to run for a second term, which he won.

By 1972 federal measures preventing voter discrimination were in full effect, and any Louisiana black who really desired to vote could do so. The election of that year was similar to others in that it pitted a North Louisiana Protestant against a South Louisiana Catholic, but there was a difference in the simple fact that the Catholic won. It also happened that winner Edwin Edwards was a moderate on the race question and sought the votes of blacks and of organized labor. The pattern of voting in North Louisiana, at least among whites, did not change; the change came in the fact that South Louisiana was more unified than ever before in support of one of its own, and population shifts had turned the tables so that South Louisiana was far more powerful than North Louisiana at the polls. Perhaps more important, the second Reconstruction had succeeded in doing what the first had failed to do: it gave real political equality to the black people of Louisiana. Edwards was re-elected in 1976.

Agriculture remained prominent despite the growth of extractive industry. Sugar continued to be the staple of the south-central part of the state, but the sugar-production system had changed considerably. In the first place, sugar-growing in the second half of the twentieth century had become a highly mechanized agricultural operation. No need existed for most of the laborers who had lived on plantations earlier in the century. Sugar cane is now planted by machine and cultivated by tractor-drawn cultivators. Harvesting is done by mechanical cane-cutters that straddle the rows and lay the cane neatly alongside, to be defoliated by tractor-mounted flame throwers. It is then mechanically picked up and loaded aboard special vehicles that transport it to the mill.

Rice, the last staple to be introduced to Louisiana, was more highly mechanized than existing crops when it came. In the 1970s, rice was planted by airplanes, which also spread chemicals inhibiting the growth of grass and weeds. Like sugar, rice has always demanded a large investment in land and machinery and has had to be cultivated on a large scale to be economically worthwhile. Rice could be grown on almost any of the arable flatlands in Louisiana, but it has been confined largely to the prairie regions of the southwest. It was for some time the main export of the Port of Lake Charles.

Cotton has continued in most years to be the major money crop of Louisiana, but cotton planting has become far different from what it was as late as the middle of the twentieth century. During the 1930s, the acreage reduction measures of the New Deal displaced many sharecroppers, and tractors began to replace mules as the motive power for implements used in cultivating cotton. During World War II, the migration of farm workers, black and white, to the North and West became massive, and it continued after the war was over. Soon after the war, growers could buy chemicals that prevented the germination of grass seed in cotton fields, making it feasible to use mechanical cotton pickers, so that the scarcity of labor resulting from the workers' exodus was not a serious inconvenience to cotton planters; cotton became as completely mechanized as sugar or rice.

After World War II, a fourth crop began to attract attention in Louisiana, and it grew in importance as the years passed. It was found that soybeans could be planted in either rice, sugar, or cotton areas, and that they require relatively little cultivation. The demand for them has increased steadily, and prices have been good. One unfortunate result of this new staple has been the clearing of thousands of acres of hardwood forest so that the land could be planted to soybeans. Since hardwoods support much of the state's wildlife, economic growth has taken an ecological toll. And as the planting of soybeans has increased, the planting of corn has declined: it is no longer a major factor in the diet of Louisianians, and the mules that once consumed most of it no longer exist.

Lumbering has become as much agriculture as industry in modern Louisiana. For a time, much cut-over land remained, for all practical purposes, abandoned, but many of the lumber companies began a program of replanting. At the same time many small tracts of land once cultivated in row crops were planted in pine seedlings. The use of pine in the making of paper has apparently created a limitless market for such pulpwood. Paper mills are scattered over the state, bringing prosperity to landowners and jobs to workers, but the stench produced by their operations has made breathing a miserable task for miles in whatever direction the wind happens to be blowing.

The production of petroleum and natural gas has come to be the state's greatest source of wealth in the twentieth century. Though some are small, almost a thousand oil fields have been developed in Louisiana. In addition, the shallow waters off the coast in the Gulf of Mexico are dotted with oil rigs. In one watery area south of Cameron, there are so many wells that it is referred to by fishermen as "Oil City." Each year the drillers have moved into deeper water, but wells beyond the three-mile limit are under federal control. The prominence of oil as a source of state revenue has posed a real danger for the future; although no one knows how much more oil remains under Louisiana, it certainly is not an unlimited amount, and one day it will be exhausted. In the 1970s, Louisiana's sulphur mines, once an important source of revenue and employment, have almost ceased to produce.

The availability of petroleum and natural gas, plus an abundant supply of fresh water and cheap water transportation have led to the growth of giant petrochemical industries. From its beginning with the Standard Oil Refinery in 1909, the industrial area of Baton Rouge has stretched northward up the left bank of the Mississippi River for miles. To the south, the river bank from Baton Rouge to New Orleans has become lined with one plant after another. Most of them use oil in one capacity or another, but among them are aluminum producers and producers of oilfield equipment. Important industrial areas also exist at Monroe, Shreveport, Morgan City, and Lake Charles, where a ship channel to the Gulf has encouraged the building of petrochemical and other plants.

New Orleans remains the state's most important port, but in the 1970s, Baton Rouge, almost a hundred miles up the Mississippi from New Orleans and thus almost two hundred miles from the Gulf, ranked thirteenth among the ports of the nation. Discussion of salt-water shipping should not be allowed to obscure the importance of fresh-water transportation to Louisiana. The Mississippi and its tributaries give access to almost all of the interior United States and to the Great Lakes. Hundreds of times as many tons of cargo moved up and down the Mississippi in the 1970s as were moved in the heyday of the river steamer. In addition, the intercoastal canal has provided a sheltered waterway for barge traffic along the coast from Brownsville, Texas, to New Jersey.

Tourism is an important source of wealth for Louisianians. Most tourists make their way to New Orleans. The Vieux Carré is unique in America, and the Crescent City boasts some of the finest restaurants in the land. The height of tourism in New Orleans begins each year with the celebration of Mardi Gras, in February, but the annual Sugar Bowl football game attracts almost as many visitors. Old plantation homes in various parts of the state draw tourists, and the legendary Evangeline Country along and near Bayou Teche is a popular attraction. People from the rest of the United States come to Louisiana for fresh- and salt-water fishing and for hunting, especially of waterfowl.

It must be emphasized once more that most Louisiana industry is extractive. In the case of lumbering, the natural resource used is renewable, with careful management, but petroleum and natural gas were millions of years in the making and once gone are gone forever. Even so, they have added tremendously to the wealth of the state, bringing a prosperity undreamed of by the average Louisianian of a century ago—or even a half century ago. Much of that wealth goes for private gratification, but it has made possible significant advances in culture and education.

By the bicentennial year of the United States, Louisiana's blacks have achieved a degree of equality that would have been unbelievable a quarter century earlier. The Negro who can afford it has access to practically all public places, the few exceptions being rural or small-town establishments whose owners knowingly defy the law and who are not worth a lawsuit. Politically, the black vote exists on a real basis of equality. More and more towns are electing black officials; blacks already sit in the legislature, and almost cerainly more will do so. Ironically, however, in the place where it began, the schools, integration apparently is failing. The completely all-white public school is a thing of the past, and faculties are thoroughly integrated. The all-black school still exists, however, and the movement of people out of the cities and even the small towns to avoid predominantly black schools and the transfer of children from public, integrated schools to private or parochial schools with no black students, or only a token few, has increased the number of all-black schools. No solution to the problem has been discovered; the Louisianian could, perhaps, take some wry comfort from the

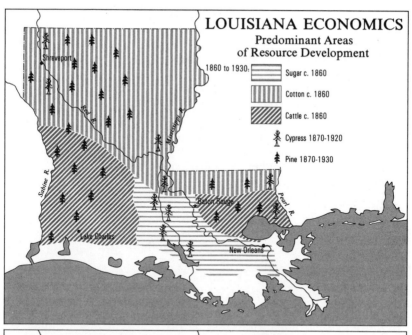

LOUISIANA ECONOMICS
Predominant Areas
of Resource Development

1860 to 1930:

Sugar c. 1860

Cotton c. 1860

Cattle c. 1860

Cypress 1870-1920

Pine 1870-1930

Shreveport

Red R.

Sabine R.

Mississippi R.

Baton Rouge

Pearl R.

Lake Charles

New Orleans

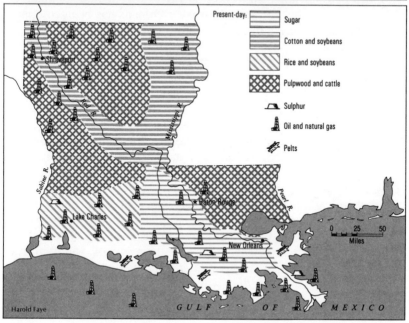

Present-day:

Sugar

Cotton and soybeans

Rice and soybeans

Pulpwood and cattle

Sulphur

Oil and natural gas

Pelts

Shreveport

Red R.

Sabine R.

Mississippi R.

Baton Rouge

Pearl R.

Lake Charles

New Orleans

0   25   50
Miles

Harold Faye

GULF   OF   MEXICO

fact that the same situation existed in the 1970s in the northern cities of the United States.

The Louisiana of 1976 is far different from the state that remained almost unchanging from the end of Reconstruction through the first quarter of the twentieth century. The small farmer has almost disappeared from the scene, as has the traditional sharecropper. For a family to maintain a small farm, it is essential for one or more members of that family to work in some industry or other nonfarm enterprise. As agriculture has become more and more mechanized, hundreds of thousands of Louisiana blacks have migrated to the cities of the North and the West. The number of black people in the state has declined by more than half in proportion to the whole; those who remain are either skilled or semiskilled agricultural laborers or town dwellers.

Tens of thousands of whites, particuarly from rural North Louisiana, also have migrated to other states. Farm families that did not leave the state tended to move to the rapidly growing cities of Louisiana. Sheveport and Baton Rouge have expanded most rapidly, but the growth of New Orleans has been comparable if those living adjacent to but not within the city proper are counted. The typical Louisianian of the bicentennial year lives in a town, but he has not been there all is life. His attitudes have remained rural—a fact to be remembered if the state is to be understood.

Thousands of people from North Louisiana moved to South Louisiana. Population in many northern parishes and in some rural areas east of the Mississippi either has remained stationary or shown a decline. All the parishes of South Louisiana have continued to grow. Opportunities for industrial employment in the 1970s have been greater in the south, especailly in petrochemical industries, which encourage natives to stay at home and also encourage immigration. Equally important, however, is the fact that the Cajuns of South Louisiana have always demonstrated great reluctance to leave their homes and families. Landholdings have been divided and subdivided until rural areas have houses on lots that would be narrow in a city. Along Bayou Lafourche there are homes so close together, so the story goes, that a baseball could be thrown from house to house for more than a hundred miles. An extremely important result of the growth of population in the south in comparison to most parishes of the north has been the shift in the political balance of power.

Such economic and demographic changes have been accompanied by cultural changes. Narrow, puritanical, evangelical Protestantism has not disappeared from the northern part of the state, but it has most definitely been eroded as rural churches have grown weaker and city churches stronger. Prohibition under local option and the sincere belief that dancing is a trap set by the devil has persisted in many areas, but such beliefs are not nearly so widespread as they were even a half century ago. In most North Louisiana towns, liquor stores flourish, and bars are not uncommon. It should be added that, in those areas where the sale of liquor is illegal, a phone call to the local bootlegger can provide what is needed, day or night.

As South Louisiana has grown in population and in political power, English has begun to replace the French language. Louisiana French ceased to be a written language about the turn of the century, but for some time local dialects, black and white, continued to be spoken. As the century wears on, however, inability to speak English, and even the ability to speak Louisiana French, have come to be considered marks of social and cultural inferiority. In the 1950s, students in college often spoke only English, or at least denied that they could speak French. Their parents were definitely bilingual. Often their grandparents spoke only French. Men and women who speak only French could still be found in the 1970s, but commonly far back on the lesser rivers and bayous; bilingual persons are not nearly so common as once was the case.

Very recently, concerned people in and out of government have suddenly realized that the disappearance of French from Louisiana would be a cultural tragedy. New interest has sprung up in once-despised Cajun speech, folklore, and music. A program was instituted, using teachers from France in many instances, to teach French to children in Louisiana elementary schools. Much has already been lost, but possibly the best of

Louisiana's French culture will yet be preserved for future generations.

One side of French culture most definitely has been preserved; Creole and Cajun cuisine still flourishes. The expert can sometimes make a distinction between the two, but largely they are inseparable. A gourmet could spend weeks sampling the specialties of various eating places in New Orleans, large and small, elegant and plain, costly and inexpensive, and have a wonderful time so doing. Excellent Creole restaurants are also to be found in most of the smaller towns of South Louisiana, and their number seems to be growing.

Even so, it is the food served in people's homes that demonstrates the survival of French cooking. Much of it is seafood, as so much of South Louisiana is on or near salt or fresh water. Crab and shrimp are enjoyed as much in Louisiana as anywhere else in the United States, but crayfish, though found throughout most of the nation, are a major delicacy only in the Pelican State. Most crayfish are boiled whole, with plenty of spice; then the tails are peeled by hand at the table, dipped in a savory sauce, and eaten until there are no more; but crayfish stew, crayfish etouffé, and above all, crayfish bisque are delicacies fit for a convention of emperors. Naturally, more prestigious fish are also eaten; redfish court bouillon demands separate mention, and although it is not exactly fish, turtle sauce piquante would titillate any civilized palate. Not all meals are of fish. A Creole or Cajun cook can do anything with a chicken that could be done anywhere else in America and can add chicken gumbo to the list. Any outlander ever invited to partake of rabbit jambalaya should not let the opportunity slip away. One of the best South Louisiana dishes is one of the plainest: beans and rice. A good South Louisiana cook can make gumbo out of almost anything—and everything. Gumbo made from wildfowl is especially prized, but so are shrimp gumbo and crab gumbo. In every case, a rich broth is served in a bowl with rice, and filé, a seasoning and thickener made of dried tender green leaves of the sassafras tree, is sprinkled over the surface. With a large chunk of French bread, this is fare fit for any gourmet and without doubt one of the most filling meals ever put on a table.

Louisiana has had a higher heart-attack rate than adjacent states, and it is quite possible that diet has been responsible for it; if so, the exchange is not unfair.

South Louisiana has had its own Cajun music, and in the northern part of the state the country-and-western music popular in the rest of the South has been preferred by rural people, in town and out. In New Orleans, birthplace of jazz and the blues, probably the best Dixieland jazz anywhere can be heard in the French Quarter, though not necessarily on Bourbon Street. Shreveport, Baton Rouge, Lake Charles, and a number of other cities have symphony orchestras, and the New Orleans symphony is recognized as one of the better ones in the nation. Opera is still staged in New Orleans, but to a limited extent, and the legitimate theater plays a much smaller role than formerly. Some compensation is found in the numerous little theater companies and the thriving departments of music and drama in the states' universities and colleges.

Louisiana has inspired much writing, but probably the best of it has been done by people who did not make their homes in the state. Probably no popular Louisiana writer of the twentieth century could be considered equal to George Washington Cable, whose work was mainly in the previous century; but Lyle Saxon, Roark Bradford, Robert Tallant, and Harnett Kane have enjoyed national as well as local reputations. A noteworthy contribution to literature was the *Southern Review,* established at Louisiana State University in the mid-1930s by Robert Penn Warren and Cleanth Brooks, Jr. It must also be noted that Robert Penn Warren's great novel, *All the King's Men,* was without question inspired by the life and death of Huey Long. Perhaps the best Louisiana writing of the twentieth century has been in history. The *Journal of Southern History* was originally established at Louisiana State University as the organ of the Southern Historical Association. The *Louisiana Historical Quarterly* was for more than a generation one of the best state historical publications, and since 1960 the Louisiana Historical Association has published *Louisiana History,* which has done much to keep interest in the history of the state alive. Able Louisiana historians of the 1970s are numerous, but special

mention should be made of Edwin Adams Davis, who, in addition to writing books and articles, created Louisiana State University's Department of Archives, an essential collection of
source materials for Louisiana and southern history. T. Harry
Williams is not primarily a historian of Louisiana, but his
P. G. T. Beauregard, Napoleon in Gray, and his Pulitzer Prize-
winning *Huey Long* deal with Louisiana subjects.

Public education in Louisiana has changed radically since the
turn of the century; then it was a stepchild, grudgingly supported by the state and secretly opposed by many political
leaders. The state budget for public education in 1920 was
somewhat less than $14 million. Recent spending amounted to
hundreds of millions of dollars. In 1920 three out of every ten
eligible children did not attend school at all, and many of the
remainder attended for very short terms. In the 1970s, attendance was compulsory through age sixteen, and almost 900,000
children attended public schools. More than 150,000 more were
enrolled in parochial and private schools. Education is the single
largest item in the state's budget. It would seem that the dreams
of those men and women who fought for schools in the first part
of the century have been fully realized, but all is not well in the
world of Louisiana education. Voices of complaint grow louder
every year as Louisiana's illiteracy rate remains among the
highest in the nation. Too many products of the state's schools,
diplomas in hand, cannot read, cannot write a comprehensible
sentence, and cannot perform simple arithmetic computations.
No answer to that problem is in sight.

The pace of change in the last half of the twentieth century
did not leave the churches untouched. Most Louisianians, black
and white, have always been church members of greater or
lesser devotion, and they remain so. The Pentecostal and other
newer Protestant sects have accepted the technology of the new
age; their sanctuaries are no longer tents or dilapidated shacks,
but convenient buildings of modern construction provided with
central heating, air conditioning, and loud-speaker systems.
Their theology, however, remains ardently fundamentalist. The
Southern Baptist Church, with a larger membership than any
other Protestant body in Louisiana, also has prospered and has

been relatively unaffected by modernist religious thought. The other conventional Protestant denominations have accepted new ideas to a greater or lesser degree, but it is probably significant that these groups grew little, if at all, while the strictly fundamentalist sects have added members rapidly. The Catholics of Louisiana also felt the winds of change following Vatican II, and many middle-aged Catholics professed to be bewildered by what went on in their churches.

Here this narrative comes to an end, but the history of Louisiana goes on.

Epilogue

*T*WO hundred and seventy-seven years have passed since Iberville's ragged band established Fort Maurepas to begin Louisiana's history as a part of the modern world. As colonizers the French failed miserably in Louisiana; but in establishing a culture they succeeded almost beyond belief. French culture, reinforced to some extent by the arrival of the Acadians, overcame German, Spanish, and African culture. The Americans who began coming in the late eighteenth century and who flooded in after 1803 were not overcome by Gallic language and customs, but they were influenced. The Spaniards were much more successful as colonial administrators than the French had been, but hindsight makes it obvious that Spain fought a holding action in Louisiana, seeking unsuccessfully to bar first English and then American expansion westward.

After 1803, Louisiana became American rapidly. The state was controlled by men of Anglo-American ancestry or descendants of the older inhabitants who adapted to Anglo-American customs and institutions. George Washington Cable's Creoles, and the Acadians of the Attakapas and other remote areas, who clung to the old ways, were bypassed, and they had little or no part in determining their destiny. Obviously, the black slaves had no voice, but the Anglo-American who was poor had little more. The state was operated for the benefit of the merchant-planter class. Even though that class led Louisiana into the disaster of the Civil War, it resumed its control after Reconstruction was over. The poor farmers remained poor, and blacks working as laborers on sugar plantations or as sharecroppers in the cotton fields were little better off than when they had been slaves. That state of affairs continued through the last third of the nineteenth century and well into the twentieth. Efforts to bring about change were crushed, one after the other.

Change finally came with the advent of Huey Long, but the long-delayed revolution brought with it excesses that negated some desirable achievements. The Long era did not, however, bring corruption to Louisiana; corruption has been more or less institutionalized in Louisiana politics since the colonial period. Institutionalized corruption exists in other states, of course, but Louisianians seem more open in acknowledging the role of the unethical and even dishonest in the governmental process. Probably it could be accurately said that Louisiana politics operates under a different set of ethics.

The twentieth century has seen Louisiana come into the mainstream of American life. Industrialization, completely commercial farming, and public education on a tremendous scale are evidence of that fact. Louisiana blacks have as much political equality as they are willing to exercise, and they have made great strides in other fields. South Louisiana has retained unique features of cuisine, vestiges of the French language, Cajun music, and a certain *joie de vivre* not characteristic of the rest of the nation. The Gothic puritanism and bigotry of North Louisiana certainly have not completely disappeared. But the survivals do not alter the fact that the state has been Americanized, and to an unfortunate degree that means that it has been standardized. There is no doubt that, materially, Louisiana is a better place to live than ever before, though, like the rest of the United States, Louisiana has its poor who do not share in the general prosperity.

But prosperity is not all to the good. Although nobody would choose to go back to the time when almost everyone was poor, it cannot be denied that, in the process of becoming "Americain," Louisiana has lost something. Somehow a drive-in hamburger emporium is out of place on Bayou Lafourche, and expensive golden upholstery on the pews of a Baptist church in North Louisiana likewise is not fitting. It is monstrous that people who speak English with an unmistakable French accent should have to be taught French. Television allows politicians to reach far more voters, but the carefully prepared television script and the elaborately made-up face will never have the savor of an impromptu stump speech on a hot and sweaty day. A cotton picker is a magnificent piece of machinery, but it will never compose a chant as it makes its way down the rows. And how sad it is that at dawn in the Louisiana countryside, it is rare to hear a cock crow and impossible to hear a mule bray. Louisiana has its memories of moonlight and magnolias, and it is right that they should be preserved, but the smell of hickory smoke from a fireplace, the odor of French bread baked in a community oven, the clamor of children released from a one-room school, the sight of women and children in their bonnets and best clothes seated in a yo-boat while the father stands facing forward and rows them to mass—these, too, are things gone forever that deserve to be remembered as part of the Louisiana heritage.

Suggestions for Further Reading

Except for the outdated and unreliable works of Charles Gayarré and Alcée Fortier, there is no readable, over-all history of colonial Louisiana. Marcel Giraud's *Histoire de la Louisiane Francaise* (Paris: Presses universitaires de France, 1953, 1958) provides superb coverage of the early French period, but the two volumes published thus far bring the story only to 1717, and only the first volume has been translated into English (Baton Rouge: Louisiana State University Press, 1974). John Walton Caughey's *Bernardo de Galvez in Louisiana, 1776–1783* (Berkeley: University of California Press, 1934) is the best account of Louisiana during the American Revolution, as well as a partial biography of a fascinating individual. Jack D. L. Holmes's *Gayoso* (Baton Rouge: Louisiana State University Press for the Louisiana Historical Association, 1966), is a readable, entertaining, and accurate account of one of the later Spanish officials.

Several good books deal with antebellum Louisiana. Roger W. Shugg, *Origins of Class Struggle in Louisiana: A Social History of White Farmers and Laborers During Slavery and After, 1840–1875* (Baton Rouge: Louisiana State University Press, 1939), deals with both prewar and postwar history. J. Carlyle Sitterson in his *Sugar Country: The Cane Sugar Industry in the South, 1753–1950* (Lexington, Ky.: University of Kentucky Press, 1953) traces the development of sugar culture and manufacturing in Louisiana from its origins almost to the present day.

Edwin Adams Davis, editor, *Plantation Life in the Florida Parishes of Louisiana, 1836–1846: As Reflected in the Diary of Bennett H. Barrow* (New York: Columbia University Press, 1943) gives a superb picture of life on a larger Louisiana cotton plantation during the years indicated. Joe Gray Taylor's *Negro Slavery in Louisiana* (Baton Rouge: Louisiana Historical Association, 1963) surveys the peculiar institution as it existed in the Pelican State. Any reader interested in the life of slaves in Louisiana or the South generally should read Solomon

Northup, *Twelve Years a Slave,* edited by Sue Eakin and Joseph Logsdon (Baton Rouge: Louisiana State University Press, 1968).

Numerous works deal with the Civil War and Reconstruction in Louisiana. John D. Winters, in *The Civil War in Louisiana* (Baton Rouge: Louisiana State University Press, 1963), gives complete coverage to military and political events of the struggle in Louisiana. Charles P. Roland, *Louisiana Sugar Plantations During the American Civil War* (Leiden, Netherlands: E. J. Brill, 1957) is a brilliantly written account of the trials and tribulations of sugar planters attempting unsuccessfully to cope with contending armies, discontented slaves, and disrupted markets. A book to be read for its own sake, even by readers who have no interest in Louisiana or the Civil War, is *Brokenburn: The Journal of Kate Stone, 1861–1868,* edited by John Q. Anderson (Baton Rouge: Louisiana State University Press, 1955). Kate Stone was well educated, sensitive, observant, and a natural diarist.

More than a half-dozen published volumes deal in one way or another with Reconstruction in Louisiana, but Joe Gray Taylor's recently published *Louisiana Reconstructed, 1863–1877* (Baton Rouge: Louisiana State University Press, 1974) has been recognized by reviewers as supplanting earlier accounts of the period. However, anyone with the slightest interest in Reconstruction should read Henry Clay Warmoth, *War, Politics and Reconstruction: Stormy Days in Louisiana* (New York: McMillan, 1930). Warmoth was the carpetbagger governor of Louisiana who lived to see Huey Long so dominant. He wrote well.

Much needs to be done on the history of Louisiana since Reconstruction, but some excellent books have been published. For the late nineteenth century, we have William Ivy Hair's *Bourbonism and Agrarian Protest in Louisiana, 1877–1900* (Baton Rouge: Louisiana State University Press, 1965) and Joy Jackson's *New Orleans in the Gilded Age: Politics and Urban Progress, 1880–1896* (Baton Rouge: Louisiana State University Press for the Louisiana Historical Association, 1969). Hair demonstrates conclusively that the end of Reconstruction brought no end to corruption in Louisiana politics, and he gives a masterful account of the failure of poor farmers, black and white, to better their condition through political action. Jackson's well-written study deals with the same period, but from the point of view of New Orleans, which is almost always an interesting subject.

Many books have been written about Huey Long, but the outstanding one by far is T. Harry Williams, *Huey Long* (New York: Alfred A. Knopf, 1971). Williams is a superb writer as well as a renowned historian, and this volume deserved the Pulitzer Prize that it received. Harnett Kane's *Louisiana Hayride: The American Rehearsal for Dictatorship, 1928–1940* (New York: William Morrow and Co., 1941) is oversensational, but its descriptions of the scandals that followed Huey Long's death are the best available.

Index

Acadians: immigrants to Louisiana, 24–25, 34; settlements, 25, 35, 59; culture and folkways, 55–56; mentioned, 90, 117. *See also* Cajuns

Adams-Onís Treaty: sets Orleans boundaries, 50

Agriculture: labor shortages in, 125; as source of income, 171; mechanization, 171

—class system: planter society dominant, 59; planters as businessmen, 61; planters' power declines, 102–103; plantation holdings change, 118; merchant-planters, 129, 182–183; yeoman farmers, 59–61, 65, 90, 115; crop-lien system, 117; economic, social conditions, 139; racist feeling, 143; sharecropping and crop liens as labor-and-credit system, 115, 116, 117, 118, 125, 126–128; planter-tenant relationships, 128, 129

—crops, livestock: major crops, 28, 118, 129; cattle, 65, 67; draft animals, 67; swine, 67; corn as basic food, 68; crop production and life styles, 69; commercialization, 118; soybeans, 172. *See also* Cotton; Rice; Sugar

—organizations: Farmers' Union, 139, 140; Farmers' Alliance movement, 140

—planatation system: dominates agriculture, 26, 57; plantation numbers and size, 58; plantation homes, 61; financing, 62; the factor, 62, 129; crops grown, 63, 69; landholding patterns change, 118

Allen, Henry Watkins (governor), 97–99

Amite River: boundary, Isle of Orleans, 19

Aubry, Charles Philippe, 19–21

Banks, Gen. Nathaniel P., 92, 93–94, 102, 106

Baton Rouge: origin of name, 3; as state capital, 119, 135; importance as port, 173; mentioned, 14, 31, 35

Battle of New Orleans, 52–55

Bayou Bienvenue, 53, 54

Bayou Lafourche: German, Acadian settlements, 11, 25; mentioned, 52, 58, 70, 129

Bayou Manchac: boundary, Isle of Orleans, 19; mentioned, 9

Bayou Teche, 58, 70, 123

Bienville, Jean Baptiste le Moyne, sieur de: explores the Mississippi, 3, 6; "preserver," Louisiana colony, 7; founds New Orleans, 9; builds Fort Rosalie, 12; governor, 13; mentioned, 14, 19

Billouart, Louis, Chevalier de Kerlérec, 14, 19

Black Codes, 103, 104. *See also Code Noir;* Blacks

Blacks: percentage of state population, 58–59, 100; status, 60–61, 88, 103–104, 121; legal protection needed for, 103, 105, 111; shift in labor patterns, 115, 117. *See also* Free People of Color; Slaves

—civil, political rights, 103, 105, 111, 133, 171, 174

—in armed forces, 92–93, 95, 99

—religious life: church memberships, denominational preferences, 81, 119; establish segregated congregations, 119–120; and black leadership, 120

—suffrage and the franchise: 103–105 *passim,* 107, 114, 121, 133, 135, 136, 138, 145

—voter registration, 144, 168, 170

189